Rick Steves'

W9-BNJ-149

POCKET

BARCELONA

Rick Steves with Gene Openshaw
and Cameron Hewitt

Contents

Introduction

As Spain's second city and the capital of the Catalan people, Barcelona bubbles with life. It's a city of distinct neighborhoods, from the tangled lanes of the Barri Gòtic to the trendy boulevards of the Eixample. It has its own unmistakable "look"—ironwork balconies, flower boxes, sidewalk mosaics, and the fanciful curves of Modernista masters like Antoni Gaudí. There's groundbreaking art from Barcelona's own Pablo Picasso and Joan Miró. The cafés are filled by day, and people crowd the streets at night, popping into tapas bars for a drink and a perfectly composed bite of seafood.

Simply put, Barcelona is unique, with a language, history, and culture separate from the rest of Spain and found nowhere else. If you're in the mood to surrender to a city's charms, let it be Barcelona.

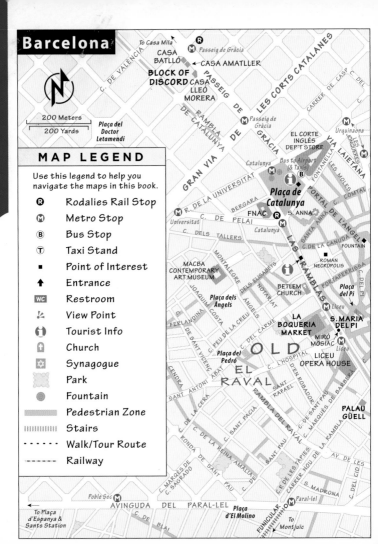

Barcelona

To Casa Mila

CASA
BATLLÓ
BLOCK OF
DISCORD
CASA
AMATLLER

CASA
LLEÓ
MORERA

Ⓡ Passeig de Gràcia
Ⓜ

C. DE VALÈNCIA

RAMBLA DE CATALUNYA

PASSEIG DE GRÀCIA

LES CORTS CATALANES

CARRER DE CASP

C. DEL

Ⓜ Passeig de Gràcia

Ⓜ Urquinaona

200 Meters
200 Yards

Plaça del Doctor Letamendi

GRAN VIA

Catalunya

EL CORTE
INGLÉS
DEP'T STORE

Bus to Airport
(& Taxis)

Ⓑ

VIA LAIETANA

FONTANELLA

MOLES

MAP LEGEND

Use this legend to help you
navigate the maps in this book.

Ⓡ   Rodalies Rail Stop

Ⓜ   Metro Stop

Ⓑ   Bus Stop

Ⓣ   Taxi Stand

▪   Point of Interest

↟   Entrance

WC   Restroom

↳   View Point

ⓘ   Tourist Info

⛪   Church

✡   Synagogue

🟫   Park

●   Fountain

▬▬▬   Pedestrian Zone

||||||||| Stairs

- - - - -   Walk/Tour Route

-------   Railway

ⓘ

**Plaça de
Catalunya**

R. DE LA UNIVERSITAT

BERGARA

Ⓜ

FNAC

Ⓡ

S. ANNA

Universitat

C. DE PELAI

Catalunya

PORTAL DE L'ANGEL

SANTA ANNA DE LA CANUDA

COMTAL

C. DELS TALLERS

C. DE LA CANUDA

FOUNTAIN

MACBA
CONTEMPORARY
ART MUSEUM

MONTALEGRE

DELS ELISABETS

NOTARIAT

ROMAN
NECROPOLIS

PORTAFERRISSA

Plaça
del Pi

JOAQUIM COSTA

BETLEM
CHURCH

Plaça dels
Àngels

ÀNGELS

LAS RAMBLAS

FERLANDINA

DE SANT VICENÇ

C. DEL CARME

C. PEU DE LA CREU

LA
BOQUERIA
MARKET

S. MARIA
DEL PI

Ⓜ
Liceu

Plaça del
Pedró

CENDRA

SANT ANTONI ABAT

C. L'HOSPITAL

D'EN ROBADOR

MIRÓ
MOSIAC

LICEU
OPERA HOUSE

Ⓜ
Liceu

OLD

**EL
RAVAL**

SANT
RAFAEL

RAMBLA DEL RAVAL

DE LA CERA

C. DE SANT PACIÀ

C. DE SANT PAU

SANT PAU

DE SANT PAU

C.R. DE LES TÀPIES

C. MARQUÈS DE BARBERÀ

PALAU
GÜELL

CARRER NOU DE LA RAMBLA

AV. DE LES

C. DEL CID

RONDA DE LA REINA AMÀLIA

C. MARQUÈS DE
C. SAGRADO

S. MADRONA

Ⓜ
Paral·lel

FUNICULAR

Poble Sec Ⓜ

← To Plaça
d'Espanya &
Sants Station

AVINGUDA DEL PARAL·LEL

C. DE BLAI

Plaça
d'El Molino

To
Montjuïc

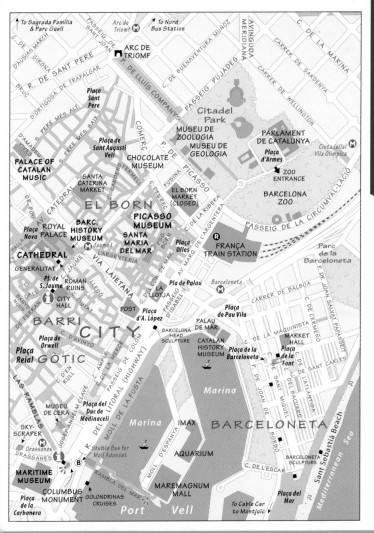

About This Book

With this book, I've selected only the best of Barcelona—admittedly, a tough call. The core of the book is six self-guided tours that zero in on Barcelona's greatest sights and neighborhoods.

My Ramblas Ramble introduces you to this lively city with a walk down one of Europe's great people-watching boulevards. The Barri Gòtic Walk and Cathedral of Barcelona Tour lay the historical groundwork for your exploration of the area's atmospheric lanes and courtyards. At the Picasso Museum, you can see how the artist's formative years in Barcelona shaped his illustrious career. The Eixample Walk focuses on the city's colorful legacy of Modernisme, while showing off the upscale side of Barcelona. Finally, there's Sagrada Família, the epic unfinished church begun by Gaudí whose prickly spires have become a symbol of the city.

The rest of the book is a traveler's tool kit. You'll find plenty more about Barcelona's attractions, from shopping to nightlife to enjoying Barcelona's tapas bars. And there are helpful hints on saving money, avoiding crowds, getting around town, enjoying a great meal, and more.

Barcelona by Neighborhood

The city of Barcelona slopes gently down a hillside to the sea. In the center sits Plaça de Catalunya, a large square that divides Barcelona into the Old City (south of the square) and new (north). Barcelona is huge and sprawling (1.6 million people), but—thanks to its walkable historic core and good public transit—all is manageable.

Think of Barcelona as a series of neighborhoods cradling major landmarks:

Plaça de Catalunya and the Ramblas: The huge, modern, central square—where all Catalunya gathers for major demonstrations—is home to big department stores, tourist services, public transportation, and convenient hotels. From here, the lively pedestrian drag called the Ramblas runs down to the harbor, past a colorful market, shops, restaurants, and street performers. To the west of the Ramblas lies the (unimportant-to-tourists) Raval neighborhood. To the east is the...

Barri Gòtic: With the cathedral as its navel, the Barri Gòtic (BAH-ree GOH-teek, Gothic Quarter) is the historic core of the Old City. It's a labyrinth of narrow streets that's ideal for strolling, shopping, dining on a pleasant square, and people-watching.

Key to This Book

Sights are rated:

▲▲▲ **Don't miss**
▲▲ **Try hard to see**
▲ **Worthwhile if you can make it**
No rating **Worth knowing about**

Tourist information offices are abbreviated as **TI,** and bathrooms are **WCs.**

Like Europe, this book uses the **24-hour clock.** It's the same through 12:00 noon, then keep going: 13:00 (1:00 p.m.), 14:00 (2:00 p.m.), and so on.

For **opening times,** if a sight is listed as "May–Oct daily 9:00–16:00," it should be open from 9 a.m. until 4 p.m. from the first day of May until the last day of October (but expect exceptions).

For **updates** to this book, visit www.ricksteves.com/update. For a valuable list of reports and experiences—good and bad—from fellow travelers, check www.ricksteves.com/feedback.

El Born: Farther east (across Via Laietana) is this rough-but-gentrifying district of shops, bistros, and nightlife, anchored by the Picasso Museum and Church of Santa Maria del Mar.

Harborfront: Modernized for the 1992 Olympics, the waterfront area has a pleasant marina and shopping mall. Farther afield is the quaint neighborhood of Barceloneta (with great seafood restaurants) and a gorgeous man-made beach.

Eixample: North of Plaça de Catalunya, the elegant Eixample (eye-SHAM-plah) district has a grid street-plan of wide boulevards lined with chic tapas bars. Along its main axis, Passeig de Gràcia, are two Modernista highlights: the "Block of Discord" and Casa Mila.

Montjuïc: The large hill overlooking the harbor to the southwest is Montjuïc (mohn-jew-EEK). Its park-like setting is home to a panoramic castle, some excellent museums (Catalan Art, Joan Miró), and the Olympic Stadium. At the base of Montjuïc, stretching toward Plaça d'Espanya, is a complex of buildings, fountains, and vistas that showcase Barcelona today.

Barcelona's Neighborhoods

North of the Center: Beyond walking distance (but easily accessible by taxi, bus, or Metro) are Gaudí's Sagrada Família and Park Güell, the viewpoint hill of Tibidabo, and the artsy Gràcia district (north of Avenue Diagonal).

Cultural Orientation to Catalunya

Besides getting oriented geographically, it's wise to acquaint yourself with Barcelona's cultural landscape. Though part of Spain politically, the city and its region (Catalunya, or Cataluña) have a different language, heritage, and outlook.

All Barcelonans speak Spanish, but three-quarters prefer the local language, Catalan. If you know Spanish, by all means use it, but try to learn at least a handful of Catalan phrases: Please (*Si us plau;* see oos plow), thank you (*gracies,* GRAH-see-es), and more (✪ see page 189).

Culturally, Catalunya is *not* the land of bullfighting, flamenco, and other Spanish clichés. It has its own calendar of local festivals, and its music, cuisine, and culture are more Mediterranean, European, and modern than they are traditionally Spanish.

Historically, Catalunya has run a parallel, independent course to the rest of Spain. Founded as a Roman retirement colony, it grew into a maritime power in the Middle Ages. These were its glory days, when the kingdom of Catalunya dominated the Mediterranean, and its unique culture was established. Then—when the rest of Spain discovered new trade routes to the Americas and entered its Golden Age—Catalunya declined. For centuries, it languished under the thumb of the central Spanish government in Madrid, which suppressed its language, government, and culture. In the 19th century, Catalunya had a rebirth (Renaixença), fueled by Industrial Age factories and creative geniuses like Gaudí who redesigned the city in Modernista style.

Today Catalunya cobbles together all these elements into a one-of-a-kind culture. On patriotic holidays, Catalunyans proudly take to the streets in the hundreds of thousands to demand greater autonomy from Madrid. You'll see Catalan symbolism in its red-and-gold-striped flag and images of the region's patron saint, the dragon-slaying St. George ("Jordi"). And citizens still gather in front of the cathedral to join hands and dance the local folk dance, the *sardana.*

Introduction

Daily Reminder

Sunday: Most sights are open, but the Boqueria and Santa Caterina markets are closed. Some sights close early today, including the Catalan Art Museum, Fundació Joan Miró, Olympic and Sports Museum, and Camp Nou Stadium (all close at 14:30), along with the Chocolate Museum (closes at 15:00). Informal performances of the *sardana* national dance take place in front of the cathedral at noon (none in Aug). Some museums are free at certain times: Catalan Art Museum and Palau Güell (free on first Sun of month); Picasso Museum and Barcelona History Museum (free on first Sun of month plus other Sun from 15:00); and the Frederic Marès Museum (free every Sun from 15:00). The Magic Fountains come alive on summer evenings (May-Sept).

Monday: Many sights are closed, including the Picasso Museum, Catalan Art Museum, Palau Güell, Barcelona History Museum, *Santa Eulàlia* schooner (at the Maritime Museum), Fundació Joan Miró, Frederic Marès Museum, Shoe Museum, Roman Temple of Augustus, and Olympic and Sports Museum. But most major Gaudí sights are open today, including the Sagrada Família, Casa Milà, Park Güell, and Casa Batlló.

Planning Your Time

Barcelona is big, so plan your time carefully, carving up the metropolis into manageable sightseeing neighborhoods. These day plans give a sense of how much an energetic traveler can see in a few days:

Day 1: In the cool of the morning, follow my Barri Gòtic Walk and Cathedral of Barcelona Tour. Do my Ramblas Ramble, then grab lunch in El Born or the Barri Gòtic. In the afternoon, tour the Palace of Catalan Music in El Born (advance reservation required). Trace my El Born walk (✪ see page 115), stopping off to do the Picasso Museum Tour. For dinner, either wait to dine at a restaurant when locals do (around 21:00) or bar-hop for tapas in El Born.

Day 2: This is Modernisme Day. Start with my Eixample Walk, touring Casa Milà and/or Casa Batlló. Eat an early lunch, then take a taxi or bus to the Sagrada Família. In the later afternoon, choose either Park Güell,

Tuesday: All major sights are open.

Wednesday: All major sights are open. The CaixaForum may be open until 23:00 in July and August.

Thursday: All major sights are open. Fundació Joan Miró is open until 21:30 year-round, and the Magic Fountains spout on summer evenings (May-Sept).

Friday: All major sights are open. The Magic Fountains light up Montjuïc year-round.

Saturday: All major sights are open. Barcelonans dance the *sardana* most Saturdays at 18:00, and the Magic Fountains dance all year.

Late-Hours Sightseeing: Sights with **year-round** evening hours (19:30 or later) include the Picasso Museum, Park Güell, CaixaForum, Columbus Monument, Cathedral of Barcelona, Casa Batlló, Las Arenas, Church of Santa Maria del Mar, and Maritime Museum (only temporary exhibits open while permanent exhibits undergo restoration, likely through 2014).

Sights offering later hours only in **peak season** (roughly April-Sept) include the Sagrada Família, Casa Milà, Palau Güell, Fundació Joan Miró, Castle of Montjuïc, and Gaudí House.

or head to Plaça de Catalunya and stroll down the Ramblas again—the scene constantly changes—and visit sights near the waterfront (Columbus Monument, mall, boat ride, maritime museum). In the evening, visit a sight that's open late (for a list, ✪ see above), take in a concert, or watch the illuminated Magic Fountains at Plaça de Espanya.

Day 3 and Beyond: Tour Montjuïc from top to bottom, stopping at the Catalan Art Museum, Fundació Joan Miró, CaixaForum art gallery, and Las Arenas (the bullring mall). In the afternoon, if the weather is good, spend the rest of the day at Barceloneta—stroll the promenade, hit the beach, have a seafood dinner, and enjoy the area's nightlife. If the beach isn't your thing, you could tour more sights (Palau Güell, Barcelona History Museum, Frederic Marès Museum), or take a walking or bike tour.

If you have more days, there are several tempting day trips, including the mountaintop monastery of Montserrat, the beach resort town of

Barcelona at a Glance

▲▲▲**Ramblas** Barcelona's colorful, gritty, tourist-filled pedestrian thoroughfare. **Hours:** Always open. See page 15.

▲▲▲**Picasso Museum** Extensive collection offering insight into the brilliant Spanish artist's early years. **Hours:** Tue-Sun 10:00-19:50, closed Mon. See page 63.

▲▲▲**Sagrada Família** Gaudí's remarkable, unfinished church—a masterpiece in progress. **Hours:** Daily April-Sept 9:00-20:30, Oct-March 9:00-18:30. See page 93.

▲▲**Palace of Catalan Music** Best Modernista interior in Barcelona. **Hours:** Fifty-minute English tours daily every hour 10:00-15:00, plus frequent concerts. See page 114.

▲▲**Casa Milà** Barcelona's quintessential Modernista building and Gaudí creation. **Hours:** Daily March-Oct 9:00-20:00, Nov-Feb 9:00-18:30. See page 121.

▲▲**Park Güell** Colorful park at the center of an unfinished Gaudí-designed housing project. **Hours:** Daily 10:00-20:00. See page 130.

▲▲**Catalan Art Museum** World-class showcase of this region's art, including a substantial Romanesque collection. **Hours:** Tue-Sat 10:00-19:00, Sun 10:00-14:30, closed Mon. See page 127.

▲▲**CaixaForum** Modernista brick factory now occupied by cutting-edge cultural center featuring excellent temporary art exhibits. **Hours:** Mon-Fri 10:00-20:00, Sat-Sun 10:00-21:00, July-Aug open late on some days—likely Wed until 23:00. See page 128.

▲**La Boqueria Market** Colorful but touristy produce market, just off the Ramblas. **Hours:** Mon-Sat 8:00-20:00, best mornings after 9:00, closed Sun. See page 25.

▲**Palau Güell** Exquisitely curvy Gaudí interior and fantasy rooftop. **Hours:** April-Sept Tue-Sun 10:00-20:00, Oct-March Tue-Sun 10:00-17:30, closed Mon year-round. See page 110.

▲**Plaça Reial** Stately square near the Ramblas, with palm trees, Gaudí-designed lampposts, and a fine slice-of-life look at Barcelona. **Hours:** Always open. See page 29.

▲**Maritime Museum** A sailor's delight, housed in an impressive medieval shipyard (but permanent collection likely closed through 2014). **Hours:** Temporary exhibits daily 10:00-20:00. See page 111.

▲**Cathedral of Barcelona** Colossal Gothic cathedral ringed by distinctive chapels. **Hours:** Generally open to visitors Mon-Fri 8:00-19:30, Sat-Sun 8:00-20:00. See page 53.

▲*Sardana* **Dances** Patriotic dance in which proud Catalans join hands in a circle, often held outdoors. **Hours:** Every Sun at 12:00, usually also Sat at 18:00, no dances in Aug. See page 112.

▲**Barcelona History Museum** One-stop trip through town history, from Roman times to today. **Hours:** Tue-Sat 10:00-19:00, Sun 10:00-20:00, closed Mon. See page 114.

▲**Santa Caterina Market** Fine market hall built on the site of an old monastery and updated with a wavy Gaudí-inspired roof. **Hours:** Mon 7:30-14:00, Tue-Wed and Sat 7:30-15:30, Thu-Fri 7:30-20:30, closed Sun. See page 117.

▲**Barcelona's Beaches** Fun-filled, man-made stretch of sand reaching from the harbor to the Fòrum. **Hours:** Always open. See page 119.

▲**Block of Discord** Noisy block of competing Modernista facades by Gaudí and his rivals. **Hours:** Always viewable. See page 88.

▲**Casa Batlló** Gaudí-designed home topped with fanciful dragon-inspired roof. **Hours:** Daily 9:00-20:00. See page 120.

▲**Fundació Joan Miró** World's best collection of works by Catalan modern artist Joan Miró and his contemporaries. **Hours:** Tue-Sat 10:00-20:00 (until 19:00 Oct-June), Thu until 21:30, Sun 10:00-14:30, closed Mon year-round. See page 123.

▲**1929 World Expo Fairgrounds** Expo site at the base of Montjuïc, featuring playful Magic Fountains, impressive CaixaForum art gallery, cheesy Spanish Village, and a mall converted from a bullring. **Hours:** Grounds always open. See page 128.

Sitges, and the Salvador Dalí sights at Figueres and Cadaqués (✪ see page 132).

These are busy day-plans, so be sure to schedule in slack time for shopping, laundry, people-watching, leisurely dinners, and recharging your touristic batteries. Slow down and be open to unexpected experiences and the hospitality of the Catalunyan people.

Quick Tips: Avoid lines at a few key sights (Picasso Museum, Sagrada Família, Casa Batlló, and Casa Milà) by buying advance tickets or a sightseeing pass (✪ see page 178 for details). Learn to navigate Barcelona by Metro, taxi, or bus (including the hop-on hop-off Tourist Bus). Adapt to the Spanish eating schedule (late lunch, late dinner) or fill the gap with tapas. Barcelona stays up late, so consider an afternoon siesta to maximize energy for after dark.

Finally, remember that Barcelona itself is a great sight. Make time to wander, shop, and simply be.

I hope you have a great trip! Traveling like a temporary local and taking advantage of the information here, you'll enjoy the absolute most out of every mile, minute, and euro. I'm happy that you'll be visiting places I know and love, and meeting some of my favorite Spanish/Catalunyan people.

Happy travels! *Buen viaje!*

The Ramblas Ramble

From Plaça de Catalunya to the Waterfront

For more than a century, this walk down Barcelona's main boulevard has drawn locals and visitors alike. While its former elegance has been tacki-fied somewhat by tourist shops and fast-food joints, this promenade still has the best people-watching in town. Walk the Ramblas at least once to get the lay of the land, then venture farther afield. It's a one-hour, downhill stroll, with an easy way to get back by Metro.

 This pedestrian-only Champs-Elysées takes you from rich (at the top) to rough (at the port). You'll raft the river of Barcelonese life past a grand opera house, elegant cafés, flower stands, retread prostitutes, bra-zen pickpockets, street mimes, a colorful market, and people looking to charge more for a shoeshine than you paid for the shoes.

ORIENTATION

Length of This Walk: Allow at least an hour. With limited time, focus on the first half, from Plaça de Catalunya to Liceu.

When to Go: It's always lively. By day, you get the best of La Boqueria Market. At night, you have all Barcelona on parade.

Getting There: The walk begins at Plaça de Catalunya (Metro: Plaça de Catalunya).

La Boqueria Market: Free, Mon-Sat 8:00-20:00, best mornings after 9:00, closed Sun, Rambla 91, Metro: Liceu, tel. 933-192-584, www.boqueria.info.

Columbus Monument: Always viewable from the outside; elevator may be closed—if open, likely €4, daily May-Oct 8:30-20:30, Nov-April 8:00-20:00, Plaça del Portal de la Pau, Metro: Drassanes, tel. 933-025-224.

Eating: Touristy places are the norm here, but ✪ see page 154 for recommendations.

The Ramblas: The word "Ramblas" is plural; the street is actually a succession of five separately named segments. But street signs and addresses treat it as a single long street—"La Rambla," singular.

La Boqueria Market on the Ramblas

Plaça de Catalunya, the Tourist Bus hub

THE WALK BEGINS

▶ *Start your ramble at the top of the Ramblas, where it connects with Plaça de Catalunya.*

❶ Plaça de Catalunya

Dotted with fountains, statues, and pigeons, and ringed by grand Art Deco buildings, this plaza is Barcelona's center. The square's stern, straight lines are a reaction to the curves of Modernisme (which predominates in the Eixample district, just to the north). Plaça de Catalunya is the hub for the Metro, bus, airport shuttle, and Tourist Bus. It's where Barcelona congregates to watch soccer matches on the big screen, to demonstrate, to celebrate, and to enjoy outdoor concerts and festivals. It's the center of the world for the 10 million Catalan inhabitants of this proud region.

Geographically and historically, the 12-acre square links old Barcelona (the narrow streets to the south) with the new (the broad boulevards to the north). In the 1850s, when Barcelona tore down its medieval walls to expand the city, this square on the edge of the walls was one of the first places to be developed.

Four great thoroughfares radiate from here. The Ramblas is the popular pedestrian promenade. Passeig de Gràcia has fashionable shops and cafés (and noisy traffic). Rambla de Catalunya is equally fashionable but cozier and more pedestrian-friendly. Avinguda del Portal de l'Angel (shopper-friendly and traffic-free) leads to the Barri Gòtic.

The inverted-staircase **monument** at the Ramblas end of the square, representing the shape of Catalunya, honors its former president, Francesc

Plaça de Catalunya—heart of the region

Proud monument to a Catalunyan president

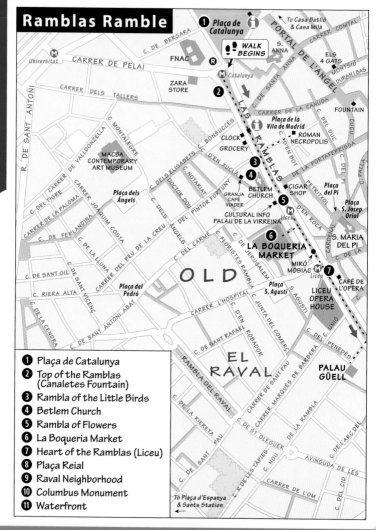

Ramblas Ramble

Map labels:

To Casa Batlló & Casa Milà
Plaça de Catalunya
WALK BEGINS
PORTAL DE L'ANGEL
S. ANNA
ELS 4 GATS
MONTSIÓ
C. COMTAL
C. DE PERGARA
Universitat
CARRER DE PELAI
FNAC
R
Catalunya
ZARA STORE
C. DE SANTA ANNA
FOUNTAIN
CARRER DELS TALLERS
C. DE LA CANUDA
C. DEL DUC
Plaça de la Vila de Madrid
ROMAN NECROPOLIS
BONSUCCÉS
CLOCK
GROCERY
C. D'EN XUCLÁ
LAS RAMBLAS
C. DE LA PORTAFERRISSA
C. PALLA
Plaça del Pi
MACBA CONTEMPORARY ART MUSEUM
DELS ELISABETS
C. NOTARIAT
DOCTOR DOU
DEL PINTOR FORTUNY
GRANJA CAFÉ VIADER
BETLEM CHURCH
CIGAR SHOP
Plaça S. Josep Oriol
Plaça dels Àngels
CARRER JOAQUÍM COSTA
C. DELS ÀNGELS
DEL CARME
CULTURAL INFO PALAU DE LA VIRREINA
LA BOQUERIA MARKET
S. MARIA DEL PI
CARRER DE VALLDONZELLA
C. DE FERLANDINA
C. DE LA LLUNA
CARRER DEL PEU DE LA CREU
OLD
FLORISTES
RAMBLA
CARRER DE JERUSALEM
MIRÓ MOSAIC
CAFÉ DE L'OPERA
C. DEL TIGRE
C. DE LA PALOMA
C. DE SANT GIL
C. DE SANT VICENÇ
Plaça del Pedró
CARRER L'HOSPITAL
C. D'EN ROBADOR
Plaça S. Agustí
S. AGUSTÍ
LICEU OPERA HOUSE
RIERA ALTA
C. DE SANT ANTONI ABAT
C. DE LA CENDRA
C. DE SANT RAFAEL
JUNTA DEL COMERÇ
EL RAVAL
C. DEL PENEDÉS
PALAU GÜELL
RAMBLA DEL RAVAL
C. DE SANT PAU
CARRER MARQUÈS DE BARBERÁ
AVINGUDA DE LES
C. DE LA RIERETA
C. DE SANT PAU
C. DE ST. OLEGUER
C. NOU
C. DE LES TÀPIES
CARRER DE L'OM
C. DEL CID
To Plaça d'Espanya & Sants Station

1. Plaça de Catalunya
2. Top of the Ramblas (Canaletes Fountain)
3. Rambla of the Little Birds
4. Betlem Church
5. Rambla of Flowers
6. La Boqueria Market
7. Heart of the Ramblas (Liceu)
8. Plaça Reial
9. Raval Neighborhood
10. Columbus Monument
11. Waterfront

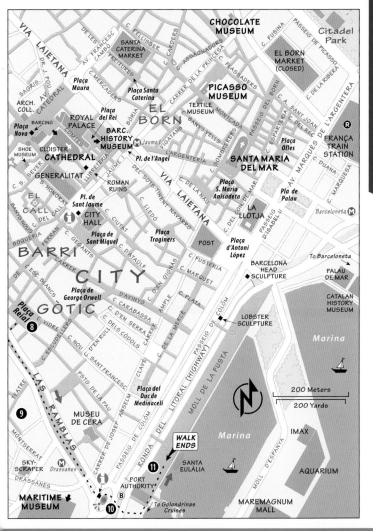

CHOCOLATE
MUSEUM

Citadel
Park

EL BORN
MARKET
(CLOSED)

VIA LAIETANA

DR. J. POU

DE LES FRANCESC

C. FELLISSER

C. CARDERS

C. FUSINA

PASSEIG DE PICASSO

AV. FRANCESC CAMBÓ

SANTA
CATERINA
MARKET

C. ASSAONADORS

C. DE LA RIBERA

C. MERCADERS

C. FREIXURES

CARRER DE LA PRINCESA

C. FLASSADERS

Plaça
Maura

Plaça Santa
Caterina

PICASSO
MUSEUM

PASSEIG DEL BORN

C. A. SANT JOAN

SAGRÉS

AV. CATEDRAL

ARCH.
COLL.

ROYAL
PALACE

EL
BORN

TEXTILE
MUSEUM

C. DEL REC

MARQUÉS DE L'ARGENTERA

Plaça
del Rei

MONTCADA

Plaça
Nova

BARCINO

C. COMTES

BARC.
HISTORY
MUSEUM

Jaume I

BANYS VELLS

Plaça
Olles

FRANÇA
TRAIN
STATION

SHOE
MUSEUM

CLOISTER

CATHEDRAL

VIGATANS

SOMBRERERS

C. ESPARTERIA

C. DUANA

C. S. SEVER

GENERALITAT

LLIBRETERIA

JAUME I

Pl. de l'Angel

L'ARGENTERIA

SANTA MARIA
DEL MAR

C. MARQUÉS

Barceloneta

EL
CALL

C. S. HONORAT

Pl. de
Sant Jaume

ROMAN
RUINS

DEL SOTSTINENT NAVARRO

Plaça
S. Maria
Anisadeta

BANYS NOUS

C. DEL CALL

CITY
HALL

C. CIUTAT

C. LLEDÓ

VIA LAIETANA

C. DE LA NAU

LA
LLOTJA

PASSEIG D'ISABEL II

BOQUERIA

FERRAN

C. GEGANTS

Plaça de
Sant Miquel

Plaça
Traginers

POST

Plaça
d'Antoni
López

To Barceloneta

PALAU
DE MAR

BARRI

CITY

C. ESC. BLANCS

CARRER

D'AVINYÓ

C. D'EN GIGNÁS

C. FUSTERIA

BARCELONA
HEAD
SCULPTURE

CATALAN
HISTORY
MUSEUM

C. D'EN SERRA

C. MARQUET

GÒTIC

Plaça de
George Orwell

C. CARABASSA

C. PLATA

Marina

Plaça
Reial

C. VIDRE

C. DELS CODOLS

PASSEIG DE COLÓM

LOBSTER
SCULPTURE

C. ESCUDELLERS

C. NOU G. SANT FRANCESC

CLAVÉ

MOLL DE LA FUSTA

N

200 Meters

200 Yards

LAS RAMBLAS

TEATRE

PSTG. DE LA PAU

Plaça del
Duc de
Medinaceli

RONDA DEL LITORAL (HIGHWAY)

Marina

IMAX

MONTSERRAT

MUSEU
DE CERA

CARRER DE JOSEP ANSELM

PASSEIG DE COLÓM

WALK
ENDS

SANTA
EULÀLIA

AQUARIUM

DRASSANES

SKY-
SCRAPER

Drassanes

PORT
AUTHORITY

To Golondrinas
Cruises

MAREMAGNUM
MALL

MARITIME
MUSEUM

Macià i Llussà, who declared independence for the breakaway region in 1931. (It didn't quite stick.) The sculptor Josep Maria Subirachs, whose work you'll see at the Sagrada Família (✪ see page 98), designed this memorial.

The venerable Café Zürich, just across the street from the monument, is a popular downtown rendezvous spot for locals. Homesick Americans might prefer the nearby Hard Rock Café.

▶ *Cross the street and start rambling down the Ramblas.*

❷ Top of the Ramblas

▶ *To get oriented, pause 20 yards down, at the ornate lamppost with a fountain as its base (on the right, near #129).*

The black-and-gold **Canaletes Fountain** has been a local favorite for more than a century. When Barcelona tore down its medieval wall and transformed the Ramblas from a drainage ditch into an elegant promenade, this fountain was one of its early attractions. Legend says that a drink from the fountain ensures that you'll come back to Barcelona one day. Watch the tourists—eager to guarantee a return trip—struggle with the awkwardly high water pressure. It's still a popular let's-meet-at-the-fountain rendezvous spot and a gathering place for celebrations and demonstrations. Fans of the Barcelona soccer team rally here before a big match—some touch their hand to their lips, then "kiss" the fountain with their hand for good luck. It's also a good spot to fill up your water bottle.

As you survey the Ramblas action, get your bearings for our upcoming stroll. You'll see the following features here and all along the way:

The wavy **tile work** represents the stream that once flowed here. *Rambla* means "stream" in Arabic, and this used to be a drainage ditch along the medieval wall of the Barri Gòtic. Many Catalan towns, established where rivers approach the sea, have streets called "Ramblas." Today Barcelona's "stream" has become a river of humanity.

Look up to see the city's characteristic shallow **balconies.** They're functional as well as decorative, with windows opening from floor to ceiling to allow more light and air into the tight, dark spaces of these cramped old buildings. The **plane trees** lining the boulevard are known for their peeling bark and hardiness in urban settings. These deciduous trees are ideal for the climate, letting in maximum sun in the winter and providing maximum shade in the summer. Nowadays, fewer residents live around here—they've been supplanted by businesses and tourism. This shapes

Canaletes Fountain—popular rendezvous spot and a good luck charm for FC Barcelona fans

what's sold along the Ramblas: There are fewer flower shops and more market stalls catering to tourists.

Nearby, notice the **chairs** fixed to the sidewalk at jaunty angles. It used to be that you'd pay to rent a chair here to look at the constant parade of passersby. Seats are now free, and it's still the best people-watching in town. Enjoy these chairs while you can—you'll find virtually no public benches or other seating farther down the Ramblas, only cafés that serve beer and sangria in just one (expensive) size: *gigante*.

Across from the fountain and a few steps down, notice the first of many **ONCE booths** along this walk (pronounced OHN-thay, the Spanish "11"). These sell lottery tickets that support Spain's organization of the blind, a powerful advocate for the needs of people with disabilities.

▶ *Continue strolling downhill.*

All along the Ramblas are **newsstands** (open 24 hours). Among their souvenirs, you'll see soccer paraphernalia, especially the scarlet-and-blue of FC Barcelona (known as "Barça"). The team is owned by its more than 170,000 "members"—fans who buy season tickets, which come with a share of ownership (the team's healthy payroll guarantees that they're always in contention). Their motto, "More than a club" *(Mes que un club),* suggests that Barça represents the entire Catalan cultural identity. This comes to a head during a match nicknamed "El Clásico," in which they face their bitter rivals, Real Madrid (whom many Barça fans view as stand-ins for Castilian cultural chauvinism).

Walk 100 yards downhill to #115, where the **Royal Academy of Science**'s clock marks official Barcelona time—synchronize. Notice the **TI** kiosk right on the Ramblas—a handy stop for any questions. The **Carrefour** supermarket just behind it has cheap groceries (at #113, Mon-Sat 10:00-22:00, closed Sun).

▶ *You're now standing at the...*

❸ Rambla of the Little Birds

Traditionally, kids brought their parents here to buy pets, especially on Sundays. Today, only a couple of these traditional pet stalls survive. For Barcelona's apartment dwellers, birds, turtles, fish, hamsters, and rabbits are easier to handle than dogs and cats.

The **street performers** you'll likely see—such as the goofy human statues—must audition and register with the city government; to avoid over-crowding, only 15 can work along the Ramblas at any one time. Dropping a

"Barca" team colors stoke regional pride

Enjoy performers, but beware pickpockets

coin in their can often kicks them into entertaining gear. Warning: Wherever people stop to gawk, pickpockets are at work.

At #122 (the big, modern Citadines Hotel on the left, just behind the first bird kiosk), a 100-yard detour through the passageway leads to a **Roman necropolis.** Look down and imagine a 2,000-year-old tomb-lined road. In Roman cities, tombs (outside the walls) typically lined the roads leading into town. Emperor Augustus spent a lot of time in modern-day Spain conquering new land, so the Romans were sure to incorporate Hispania into the empire's infrastructure. This road, Via Augusta, led into the Roman port of Barcino (today's highway to France still follows the route laid out by this Roman thoroughfare). Looking down at these ruins, you can see how Roman Barcino was about 10 feet lower than today's street level.

▶ *Return to the Ramblas and continue downhill 100 yards or so to the next street. At Carrer de la Portaferrissa (across from the big church), turn left a few steps and look right to see the **decorative tile** over the fountain. The scene shows the original city wall with the gate that once stood here and the action on what is today's Ramblas. Nearby, note the Palau de la Virreina ticket office (La Rambla 99), a good one-stop-shopping place for concerts and events. Cross the boulevard to the front of the big church.*

❹ Betlem Church

This 17th-century church is dedicated to Bethlehem, and for centuries locals have flocked here at Christmastime to see Nativity scenes.

The church's sloping roofline, ball-topped pinnacles, corkscrew columns, and scrolls above the entrance all identify it as Baroque. But compared to the rest of Baroque-crazy Spain, that style is relatively unusual in

Barcelona. During the heyday of the Renaissance and Baroque periods (about 1500-1850), Barcelona was a relatively poor city, under the repressive thumb of the central government in Madrid. Barcelona's greatest architectural legacy comes from its glory years—the medieval period and the turn of the 20th century.

For a sweet treat, head down the narrow lane behind the church (going uphill parallel to the Ramblas about 30 yards) to the recommended family-run **Café Granja Viader,** which has specialized in baked and dairy delights since 1870. Step inside to see Viader family photos and early posters advertising Cacaolat—the local chocolate milk Barcelonans love.

▶ *Continue down the boulevard, through the stretch called the...*

❺ Rambla of Flowers

This colorful block is lined with flower stands. On the left, at #100, **Gimeno** sells cigars. Step inside and appreciate the dying art of cigar boxes. Go ahead, do something forbidden in America but perfectly legal here—buy a Cuban (little singles for €1). Tobacco shops sell stamps and phone cards, plus bongs and marijuana gear—the Spanish approach to pot is very casual. While people can't legally sell marijuana, they're allowed to grow it for personal use and consume it.

▶ *Continue to the Metro stop marked by the red M. At #91 (on the right) is the arcaded entrance to Barcelona's great covered market, La Boqueria. If this main entry is choked with visitors (as it often is), you can skirt around to a side entrance, one block in either direction (look for the round arches that mark passages into the market colonnade).*

Betlem Church, a rare Baroque structure

One segment of the "Ramblas" has flowers

⑥ La Boqueria Market

This lively market hall is an explosion of chicken legs, bags of live snails, stiff fish, delicious oranges, odd odors, and sleeping dogs. The best day for a visit is Saturday, when the market is thriving. It's closed on Sundays, and locals avoid it on Mondays, when it's open but (they believe) vendors are selling items that aren't necessarily fresh.

Since as far back as 1200, Barcelonans have bought their animal parts here. The market was originally located by the walled city's entrance, as many medieval markets were (since it was more expensive to trade within the walls). It later expanded into the colonnaded courtyard of a now-gone monastery before being topped with a colorful arcade in 1850.

While tourists are drawn like moths to a flame to the area around the main entry (below the colorful stained-glass sign), explore deeper. Locals know that the stalls up front pay the highest rent—and therefore have to inflate their prices and cater to out-of-towners. For example, the juice bars along the touristy main drag charge more than those a couple of aisles to the right.

Stop by the recommended **Pinotxo Bar**—it's just inside the market, under the sign—and snap a photo of animated Juan giving a thumbs-up

La Boqueria entrance—the arcade hosts vendors of seafood, produce, and hocks of gourmet *jamón*

for your camera. The stools nearby are a fine perch for enjoying both your coffee and the people-watching.

The market and lanes nearby are busy with tempting little eateries (✪ see page 154). Drop by a café for an *espresso con leche* or breakfast *tortilla española* (potato omelet). Explore even deeper. The small square on the north side of the market hosts a farmers' market in the mornings. Wander around—as local architect Antoni Gaudí used to—and gain inspiration. Go on a scavenger hunt for some unusual items.

Produce stands show off seasonal fruits and vegetables. In the fall, you'll see lots of mushrooms; in the winter, artichokes. "Market cuisine" is big at Barcelona restaurants—chefs come to markets like this each morning to rustle up ingredients. The tubs of little green peppers that look like jalapenos are lightly fried for the dish called *pimientos de Padrón.* Olives are a keystone of the Spanish diet. Take a look at the 25 kinds offered at the **Graus Olives i Conserves** shop (straight in, near the back).

Full legs of *jamón* (ham)—some costing upwards of 200 euros—tempt the Spaniards who so love this local delicacy (✪ see page 151). You'll see many types of *chorizo* (red spicy sausage) and gamier meats such as rabbit and suckling pig. *Huevos del toro* are bull testicles—surprisingly inexpensive...and oh so good.

The fishmonger stalls could double as a marine biology lab. Count the many different types of shrimp (*gamba, scampi, langostino,* clawed *cigala*). Notice that fish is sold whole, not filleted—local shoppers like to look their dinner in the eye to be sure it's fresh. One of the weirdest Spanish edibles is the tubular razor clam *(navaja de almeja),* with something oozing out of each end. Salt cod *(bacalao)* is preserved and dried. Before it can be

Of the market's many vendors, here's Juan

The market is a photographic wonderland

Fresh seafood, base of Barcelonan cuisine

Mosaic by hometown boy Joan Miró

eaten, it must be rehydrated. Historically, this provided desperately needed protein on long sea voyages.

▶ *Head back out to the street and continue down the Ramblas.*

You're skirting the western boundary of the old Barri Gòtic neighborhood. As you walk, glance to the left through a modern cutaway arch for a glimpse of the medieval church tower of **Santa Maria del Pi,** a popular venue for guitar concerts (✪ see page 183). This also marks Plaça del Pi and a great shopping street, Carrer Petritxol, which runs parallel to the Ramblas (see the Shopping in Barcelona chapter).

At the corner directly opposite the modern archway, find the highly regarded **Escribà** bakery (look for the *Antigua Casa Figueras* sign arching over the doorway), with its fine Modernista facade and interior. Notice the beautiful mosaics, stained glass, and woodwork. On the sidewalk in front of the door, a commemorative plaque notes the business's establishment in 1902 (plaques like these identify historic shops all over town).

▶ *After another block, you reach the Liceu Metro station, marking the...*

❼ Heart of the Ramblas

At the Liceu Metro station's elevators, the Ramblas widens a bit into a small, lively square (Plaça de la Boqueria). Liceu marks the midpoint of the Ramblas, halfway between Plaça de Catalunya and the waterfront.

Underfoot in the center of the Ramblas, find the much-trod-upon red-white-yellow-and-blue **mosaic** by homegrown abstract artist Joan Miró. The mosaic's black arrow represents an anchor, a reminder of the city's attachment to the sea. Miró's stripped-down designs are found all over the city, from murals to mobiles to the La Caixa bank logo. The best place in

Barcelona to see his work is in the Fundació Joan Miró at Montjuïc (✪ see page 123).

The surrounding buildings have playful ornamentation typical of the city. The **Chinese dragon** holding a lantern (at #82) decorates a former umbrella shop (notice the fun umbrella mosaics high up). The dragon is an important symbol of Catalan pride for its connection to the city's dragon-slaying patron saint, St. George (Jordi).

Hungry? The recommended **Taverna Basca Irati** tapas bar is a block up Carrer del Cardenal Casanyes (find the street around the back side of the former umbrella shop). This is one of many user-friendly, Basque-style tapas bars in town; instead of ordering, you can just grab or point to what looks good on the display platters, then pay per piece.

Back on the Ramblas, a few steps down (on the right) is the **Liceu**

Fanciful decorations on buildings, like this one near Liceu Metro, are part of Barcelona's charm

Opera House (Gran Teatre del Liceu), which hosts world-class opera, dance, and theater (box office around the right side, open Mon-Fri 13:30-20:00). Opposite the opera house is Café de l'Opera (#74), an elegant stop for an expensive beverage. This bustling café, with Modernista decor and a historic atmosphere, boasts that it's been open since 1929, even during the Spanish Civil War.

▶ *We've seen the best stretch of the Ramblas; from here, it's downhill (in every sense, when it comes to the Raval neighborhood) to the port. To cut this walk short, you could catch the Metro back to Plaça de Catalunya.*

Otherwise, continue down the Ramblas. In about 30 yards, the wide, straight street on the left (Carrer de Ferran) leads to Plaça de Sant Jaume, the government center.

Stay on the Ramblas for another 50 yards (to #46), and turn left down an arcaded lane (Correr de Colom) to the square called...

❽ Plaça Reial

Dotted with palm trees, surrounded by an arcade, and ringed by yellow buildings with white Neoclassical trim, this elegant square has a colonial ambience. It comes complete with old-fashioned taverns, modern bars with patio seating, and a Sunday coin-and-stamp market (10:00-14:00). Completing the picture are Gaudí's first public works (the two colorful helmeted lampposts). While this used to be a seedy and dangerous part of town, recent gentrification efforts have given it new life, making it inviting and accessible. (The small streets stretching toward the water from the square remain a bit sketchier.) It's a lively hangout by day or by night

Plaça Reial—a lively hangout

Palau Güell—parabolic arches by Gaudí

(✿ see page 184). Big spaces like this (as well as the site of La Boqueria Market) often originated as monasteries. When these were dissolved in the 19th century, their fine colonnaded squares were incorporated into useful public spaces.

▶ *Head back out to the Ramblas.*

Across the boulevard, a half-block detour down Carrer Nou de la Rambla brings you to **Palau Güell,** designed by Antoni Gaudí (on the left, at #3-5). Recently renovated, Palau Güell offers an informative look at a Gaudí interior (✿ see listing on page 110). Pablo Picasso had a studio at #10 (though there's nothing to see there today).

▶ *Retrace your steps and continue downhill on the Ramblas.*

❾ Raval Neighborhood

The neighborhood on the right-hand side of this stretch of the Ramblas is El Raval. In the last century, this was a rough neighborhood, home to sailors, prostitutes, and poor immigrants. Today, it's becoming gentrified, but it's still pretty dodgy.

The seedy zone attracts plenty of characters who don't need the palm trees to be shady. You're likely to see some good old-fashioned shell games. Stand back and observe these nervous no-necks at work. They swish around their little boxes, making sure to show you the pea. Their shills play and win. Then, in hopes of making easy money, fools lose big time.

Near the bottom of the Ramblas, take note of the **Drassanes Metro stop** (close to the Museo de Cera—wax museum), which can take you back to Plaça de Catalunya when this walk is over. The skyscraper to the right of the Ramblas is the Edificio Colón. When it was built in 1970, the 28-story structure was Barcelona's first high-rise. Near the skyscraper is the Maritime Museum, housed in what were the city's giant medieval shipyards (✿ see page 111).

▶ *Up ahead is the...*

❿ Columbus Monument

The 200-foot **column** honors Christopher Columbus, who came to Barcelona in 1493 after journeying to America. This Catalan answer to Nelson's Column on London's Trafalgar Square (right down to the lions perfect for posing with at the base) was erected for the 1888 Universal

The Columbus Monument, located where the Ramblas meets the sea, honors a man with Barcelona ties

Exposition, an international fair that helped vault a surging Barcelona onto the world stage.

The base of the monument, ringed with four winged victories (taking flight to the four corners of the earth), is loaded with symbolism: statues and reliefs of mapmakers, navigators, early explorers preaching to sub-servient Native Americans, and (enthroned just below the winged victo-ries) the four regions of Spain. The reliefs near the bottom illustrate scenes from Columbus' fateful voyage. It's ironic that Barcelona so celebrates this explorer; the discoveries of Columbus started 300 years of decline for the city, as Europe began to face West (the Atlantic and the New World) rather than East (the Mediterranean and the Orient). Within a few decades of Columbus, Barcelona had become a depressed backwater, and didn't rebound until events like the 1888 Expo cemented its status as a come-back city.

A tiny four-person elevator ascends to the top of the monument (though it may be closed when you visit). When it's open, it lifts visitors to a glassed-in observation area for fine panoramas over the city (entrance/ticket desk in TI inside the base of the monument).

▸ *Scoot across the busy traffic circle to survey the...*

⓫ Waterfront

Stand on the boardwalk (between the modern bridge and the kiosks selling harbor cruises), and survey Barcelona's bustling maritime zone. Although the city is one of Europe's top 10 ports, with many busy industrial harbors and several cruise terminals, this low-impact stretch of seafront is clean, fresh, and people-friendly.

As you face the water, the frilly yellow building to your left is the fanciful Modernista-style port-authority building. The wooden pedestrian **bridge** jutting straight out into the harbor is a modern extension of the Ramblas. Called La Rambla de Mar ("Rambla of the Sea"), the bridge swings out to allow boat traffic into the marina; when closed, the footpath leads to an entertainment and shopping complex. Just to your right are the *golondri-nas* **harbor cruise** boats, which can be fun if you'd love to get out on the water (though the views from the harbor aren't great; for details, ✪ see page 112).

▸ *Turn left and walk 100 yards along the promenade between the port authority and the harbor.*

This delightful promenade is part of Barcelona's **Old Port** (Port Vell).

The port's pleasant sailboat marina is completely enclosed by a modern complex with the Maremagnum shopping mall, an IMAX cinema, a huge aquarium, restaurants, and piles of people. Along the promenade is a permanently moored historic schooner, the *Santa Eulália* (part of the Maritime Museum—✪ see page 111).

Imagine: A little more than two decades ago, this was a gloomy, depressed warehouse zone. It was refurbished for the 1992 Olympics. City leaders routed a busy highway underground to create this fine walkway sprinkled with palm trees and eye-pleasing public art.

From here, you can also pick out some of Barcelona's more distant charms. The triangular spit of land across the harbor is the neighborhood of **Barceloneta**—a somewhat gritty but charming area, popular for its easy access to an inviting stretch of broad, sandy beaches. Looking back toward the Columbus Monument, in the distance you'll see the majestic, 570-foot bluff of **Montjuïc,** dotted with a number of sights and museums (✪ see page 122).

▶ *Your ramble is over. To return to Plaça de Catalunya or to reach other points in town, your best bet is to backtrack to the Drassanes Metro stop, at the bottom of the Ramblas. Alternatively, you can catch buses #14 or #59 from along the top of the promenade.*

This wave-like pedestrian bridge over the harbor leads to the modern Maremagnum shopping mall

Barri Gòtic Walk

From Plaça de Catalunya to Plaça del Rei

Barcelona's Barri Gòtic (Gothic Quarter) is a bustling world of shops, bars, and nightlife packed into narrow, winding lanes and undiscovered courtyards. This is Barcelona's birthplace—where the ancient Romans built a city, where medieval Christians built their cathedral, and where Barcelonans lived within a ring of protective walls until the 1850s, when the city expanded.

Today, the area—"El Gòtic"—is historic and atmospheric. It's a grab bag of grand squares, classy antiques shops, wrought-iron balconies, and street musicians strumming Catalan folk songs. In the center of it all is the cathedral, surrounded by other legacy sights from the city's 2,000-year history. Use this walk to get the lay of the land, then explore the shopping streets nearby (✪ see page 181) or head to El Born (✪ see page 115).

ORIENTATION

Length of This Walk: Figure 1.5 hours, not including entering sights such as the cathedral.

When to Go: If you want to enter the cathedral, go in the morning or late afternoon, when admission is free. Some sights mentioned on this walk are closed Monday.

Getting There: Push off from the southeast corner of the Plaça de Catalunya, near El Corte Inglés department store (Metro: Plaça de Catalunya).

Church of Santa Anna: Free, hours vary but usually Mon-Sat 9:30-13:00 & 18:00-20:00, Sun 9:30-14:00, Plazoleta de Santa Anna.

Cathedral of Barcelona: Generally free except in afternoon, open Mon-Fri 8:00-19:30, Sat-Sun 8:00-20:00, €6 to enter Mon-Sat 13:00-17:00 and Sun 14:00-17:00, Plaça de la Seu.

Old Main Synagogue: €2.50, Mon-Fri 10:30-18:30, Sat-Sun 10:30-15:00, Carrer Marlet 5, tel. 933-170-790, www.calldebarcelona.org.

Roman Temple of Augustus: Free; April-Sept Tue-Sun 10:00-20:00; Oct-March Tue-Sat 10:00-14:00 & 16:00-19:00, Sun 10:00-20:00; closed Mon year-round; Carrer del Paradís 10.

Barcelona History Museum: €7, Tue-Sat 10:00-19:00, Sun 10:00-20:00, closed Mon, off Plaça del Rei.

Eating: For suggestions, ✪ see page 156.

THE WALK BEGINS

▶ *Start on Barcelona's grand main square, **Plaça de Catalunya** (✪ described on page 17 of the Ramblas Ramble chapter). From the southeast corner (between the giant El Corte Inglés department store and the Banco de España), head down the broad pedestrian boulevard called...*

❶ Avinguda del Portal de l'Angel

For much of Barcelona's history, this was one of the main boulevards leading into town. A medieval wall enclosed the city, and there was an entrance here—the "Gate of the Angel"—that gives the street its name. An angel statue atop the gate purportedly kept the city safe from plagues and bid voyagers safe journey as they left the security of the city.

The street (like many other areas of the city) got periodic facelifts whenever Barcelona held events that welcomed the world: the 1888 Universal Exposition (that also gave us the Columbus Monument), the 1929 World's Fair (that created Plaça d'Espanya), and the 1992 Olympic Games (that rejuvenated Montjuïc and the waterfront).

Today, this formerly traffic-choked street welcomes shoppers cruising the most expensive retail spaces in town. It's pretty globalized and sanitized, with lots of high-end Spanish and international chains (for a brief rundown, ✪ see page 182), but a handful of local businesses survive. At the first corner (at #21), a green sign marks **Planelles Donat**—long appreciated for its ice cream, sweet *turró* (or *turrón,* almond-and-honey candy), refreshing *orxata* (or *horchata*, almond-flavored drink), and *granissat* (or *granizado,* ice slush).

▶ *A block farther down, pause at Carrer de Santa Anna to admire the Art Nouveau awning at another El Corte Inglés department store. (If you're keeping track, this is the third El Corte Inglés within a two-block radius.) Take a half-block detour down Carrer de Santa Anna to the doorway at #29 (on the right), which leads to the...*

❷ Church of Santa Anna

This 12th-century gem, with a pleasant, flower-fragrant courtyard, was an *extra muro* ("outside the walls") church; look for its marker cross still standing outside. Because it was part of a convent, the church has a fine cloister—an arcaded walkway around a leafy courtyard (viewable through

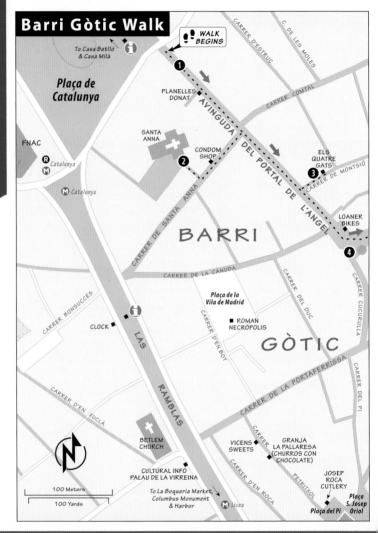

Barri Gòtic Walk

WALK BEGINS

To Casa Batlló & Casa Milà

Plaça de Catalunya

FNAC

Catalunya

Catalunya

Catalunya

PLANELLES DONAT

SANTA ANNA

CONDOM SHOP

AVINGUDA DEL PORTAL DE L'ANGEL

ELS QUATRE GATS

CARRER DE MONTSIÓ

LOANER BIKES

CARRER DE LES MOLES

CARRER D'ESTRUC

CARRER COMTAL

CARRER DE SANTA ANNA

BARRI

CARRER DE LA CANUDA

Plaça de la Vila de Madrid

ROMAN NECRÒPOLIS

GÒTIC

CARRER DEL DUC

CARRER CUCURULLA

CARRER DE LA PORTAFERRISSA

CARRER DEL PI

CLOCK

CARRER BONSUCCÈS

CARRER D'EN BOT

LAS RAMBLAS

CARRER D'EN XUCLA

BETLEM CHURCH

CULTURAL INFO PALAU DE LA VIRREINA

To La Boqueria Market, Columbus Monument & Harbor

Liceu

VICENS SWEETS

GRANJA LA PALLARESA (CHURROS CON CHOCOLATE)

CARRER D'EN ROCA

PETRITXOL

JOSEP ROCA CUTLERY

Plaça S. Josep Oriol

Plaça del Pi

100 Meters

100 Yards

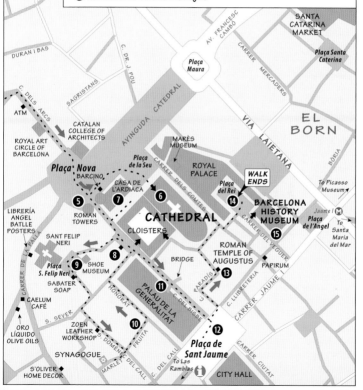

1 Avinguda del Portal de l'Angel
2 Church of Santa Anna
3 Els Quatre Gats Rest.
4 Fountain
5 Plaça Nova
6 Cathedral of Barcelona
7 Casa de l'Ardiaca
8 Monument to the Martyrs
9 Plaça Sant Felip Neri
10 Jewish Quarter
11 Carrer del Bisbe Bridge
12 Plaça de Sant Jaume
13 Roman Temple of Augustus
14 Plaça del Rei
15 Barcelona History Museum

the gate to the left of the church). If the church is open, you'll see a bare Romanesque interior and Greek-cross floor plan, topped with an octagonal wooden roof. The recumbent-knight tomb is that of Miguel de Boera, renowned admiral under Emperor Charles V. The door at the far end of the nave leads to the cloister.

As you head back to the main drag, you'll pass—a few doors down—a **condom shop** on your left. It advertises (to men with ample self-esteem): *Para los pequeños placeres de la vida*—"For the little pleasures in life."

▶ *Return to Avinguda del Portal de l'Angel, turn right, and continue for another block. At Carrer de Montsió (on the left), side-trip half a block to...*

❸ Els Quatre Gats

This restaurant ("The Four Cats"), established in 1897, is a historic monument, tourist attraction, nightspot, and one of my recommended eateries. It's famous for being the bohemian-artist hangout where Picasso nursed drinks with friends and first publicly hung his art (in 1900, at age 19). The building itself, by the prominent Catalan architect Josep Puig i Cadafalch, is a Modernista landmark. Stepping inside, you feel the turn-of-the-20th-century vibe. Rich Barcelona elites and would-be avant-garde artists looked to Paris, not Madrid, for cultural inspiration. Consequently, this place was clearly inspired by the Paris scene, especially Le Chat Noir cabaret/café, the hangout of Montmartre intellectuals. Like Le Chat Noir, Els Quatre Gats even published its own artsy magazine for a while. The story of the name? When the proprietor told his friends that he'd stay open 24 hours a day, they said, "No one will come. It'll just be you and four cats" (Catalan slang for "a few crazy people"). While you can have a snack, meal, or drink here, if you just want to look around, ask, *"Solo mirar, por favor?"*

▶ *Return to and continue down Avinguda del Portal de l'Angel. In a square on the left, notice the rack of* **city loaner bikes,** *part of the popular and successful "Bicing" program designed to reduce car traffic (available only to Barcelona residents). You'll soon reach a fork in the road and a building with a...*

❹ Fountain

The blue-and-yellow tilework, a circa-1918 addition to this even-older fountain, depicts ladies carrying jugs of water. In the 17th century, this was the last watering stop for horses before leaving town. As recently as 1940, one in nine Barcelonans got their water from fountains like this. It's still used today.

▶ *Take the left fork, down Carrer dels Arcs.*

Pause after a few steps at the yellow La Caixa ATM (on the right, under the terrace). Watch as various international languages pop up on the screen—in addition to English, French, and German, you'll see the **four languages of Spain** and their flags: Català (Catalan; thin red-and-gold stripes), Galego (Galicia, in northwest Spain; blue with a diagonal white slash), Español (Spanish; broad red, yellow, and red bands), and Euskaraz (Basque; red, green, and white). As a would-be breakaway nation fiercely proud of its own customs and language, Catalunya is particularly careful to respect linguistic variation.

Just past the ATM, you'll pass the **Royal Art Circle of Barcelona,** a private collection of Dalí sculptures (Reial Cercle Artístic de Barcelona, some temporary exhibits).

▶ *Enter the large square called...*

❺ Plaça Nova

Two bold **Roman towers** flank the main street. These once guarded the entrance gate of the ancient Roman city of Barcino. The big stones that make up the base of the (reconstructed) towers are actually Roman. Near the base of the left tower, **modern bronze letters** spell out "BARCINO." The city's name may have come from Barca, one of Hannibal's generals, who is said to have passed through during Hannibal's roundabout invasion of Italy. At Barcino's peak, the **Roman wall** (see the section stretching to the left of the towers) was 25 feet high and a mile around, with 74 towers. It enclosed an area of 30 acres and a population of 4,000.

One of the towers has a section of **Roman aqueduct** (a modern

Old tilework fountain along the Avinguda

Two ancient Roman towers on Plaça Nova

Frieze by Barcelona's own Pablo Picasso

Cathedral—medieval core, 19th-century facade

reconstruction). These bridges of stone carried fresh water from the distant hillsides into the walled city. Here the water supply split into two channels, one to feed Roman industry, the other for the general populace. The Roman aqueducts would be the best water system Barcelona would have until the 20th century.

Opposite the towers is the modern **Catalan College of Architects** building (Collegi d'Arquitectes de Barcelona), which is, ironically for a city with so much great architecture, quite ugly. The frieze was designed by Picasso (1960) in his distinctive simplified style, showing Catalan traditions: shipping, music, the *sardana* dance, bullfighting, and branch-waving kings and children celebrating a local festival. Picasso spent his formative years (1895-1904, ages 14-23) in the Barri Gòtic. He had a studio a block from here (where the big CaixaCatalunya building stands today). He drank with fellow bohemians at Els Quatre Gats and frequented brothels a few blocks from here on Carrer d'Avinyó ("Avignon")—which inspired his influential Cubist painting *Les Demoiselles d'Avignon*. Picasso's Barri Gòtic was a hotbed of trend-setting art, propelling him forward just before he moved to Paris and remade modern art.

▶ Head left through Plaça Nova and take in the mighty facade of the...

❻ Cathedral of Barcelona (Catedral de Barcelona)

This location has been a center of Christian worship since the fourth century, and this particular building dates (mainly) from the 14th century. The facade is a virtual catalog of Gothic motifs: a pointed arch over the entrance, robed statues, tracery in windows, gargoyles, and bell towers with winged angels. This Gothic variation is called French Flamboyant (meaning "flame-like"), and the roofline sports the prickly spires meant to give the impression of a church flickering with spiritual fires. The facade is typically Gothic...but not from medieval times. It's a Neo-Gothic reinterpretation from the 19th century. The area in front of the cathedral is where Barcelonans dance the *sardana* (✪ see page 112).

The cathedral's interior—with its vast size, peaceful cloister, and many ornate chapels—is worth a visit.

For a walk through the cathedral's interior, ✪ see the Cathedral of Barcelona Tour chapter.

▶ *Facing the cathedral, locate a few other attractions you may want to visit later. The* **Frederic Marès Museum**—*an eclectic collection of 19th-century slice-of-life items—is just to the left (✪ see page 113). To the far, far left is the multicolored, wavy roofline of the Santa Caterina Market, marking the edge of the* **El Born** *neighborhood (✪ see page 115). To the right of the cathedral, at the far end of the square, is Carrer de la Palla, is a good starting point for* **shopping** *in the Barri Gòtic (for recommendations, ✪ see page 181).*

For now, return to the Roman towers. Pass between the towers to head up Carrer del Bisbe, and take an immediate left, up the ramp to the entrance of the...

❼ Casa de l'Ardiaca

It's free to enter this mansion, which was once the archdeacon's residence and today functions as the city archives. The elaborately carved doorway is Renaissance. To the right of the doorway is a carved mail slot by 19th-century Modernista architect Lluís Domènech i Montaner. Enter into a small courtyard with a fountain. Notice how the century-old palm tree

Casa de l'Ardiaca's Modernista mail slot

Monument to the Martyrs of Independence

seems to be held captive by urban man. Next, step inside the lobby of the city archives. You can't tour the archives, but there are often temporary exhibits in the lobby. At the left end of the lobby, go through the archway and look down into the stairwell—this is the back side of the ancient Roman wall. Back in the courtyard, head up to the balcony for views of the cathedral steeple and gargoyles. Note the small Romanesque chapel on the right, the only surviving 12th-century bit of the cathedral.

▶ *Return to Carrer del Bisbe and turn left. After a few steps, you reach a small square with a bronze statue ensemble.*

❽ Monument to the Martyrs of Independence

Five Barcelona patriots calmly receive their last rites before being garroted (strangled) for resisting Napoleon's occupation of Spain in the early 19th century. They'd been outraged by French atrocities in Madrid (depicted in Goya's famous *Third of May* painting in Madrid's Prado Museum). According to the plaque marking their mortal remains, these martyrs to independence gave their lives in 1809 *"por Dios, por la Patria, y por el Rey"*—for God, country, and king.

The plaza offers interesting views of the cathedral's towers. Opposite the square is the "back door" entrance to the cathedral (through the cloister; relatively uncrowded but open only sporadically).

On this square (and throughout the Barri Gòtic), you're likely to see groups of hippies. Nicknamed the "dog-and-flute people," they squat together in abandoned buildings, living in communes, and spend their days begging, entertaining, and bringing chaos to otherwise peaceful demonstrations. Attracted by Barcelona's easygoing laws, they congregate here.

▶ *Exit the square down tiny Carrer de Montjuïc del Bisbe (to the right as you face the martyrs). This leads to the cute...*

❾ Plaça Sant Felip Neri

This square serves as the playground of an elementary school and is often bursting with energetic kids speaking Catalan (just a generation ago, they would have had to speak Spanish). The Church of Sant Felip Neri, which Gaudí attended, is still pocked with bomb damage from the Spanish Civil War. As a stronghold of democratic, anti-Franco forces, Barcelona saw a lot of fighting. The shrapnel that damaged this church was meant for the nearby Catalan government building (Palau de la Generalitat, which we'll see later on this walk).

The Church of Sant Felip Neri still shows bomb damage from Spain's bitter Civil War of the 1930s

Study the carved reliefs on nearby buildings, paid for by the guilds that powered the local economy. It's clear that the building on the far right must have housed the shoemakers. In fact, just next door is the entertaining little **Shoe Museum** (✪ described on page 113). Also fronting the square is the fun **Sabater Hermonos** artisanal soap shop.

▶ *Exit the square down Carrer de Sant Felip Neri. At the T-intersection, turn right onto Carrer de Sant Sever, then immediately left on Carrer de Sant Domènec del Call. You've entered the...*

❿ Jewish Quarter (El Call)

In Catalan, a Jewish quarter goes by the name El Call—literally "narrow passage," for the tight lanes where medieval Jews were forced to live, under the watchful eye of the nearby cathedral. At the peak of Barcelona's El Call, some 4,000 Jews were crammed into just a few alleys.

Walk down Carrer de Sant Domènec del Call, passing the **Zoen leather workshop and showroom,** where everything is made on the spot (on the right, at #15). After passing a charming square, also on the right, take the next lane to the right (Carrer de Marlet). On the right is the low-profile entrance to what was likely Barcelona's **Old Main Synagogue** (Antigua Sinagoga Mayor) during the Middle Ages. The structure dates from the third century, but it was destroyed during a brutal pogrom in 1391. The city's remaining Jews were expelled in 1492, and artifacts of their culture—including this synagogue—were forgotten for centuries. In the 1980s, a historian tracked down the synagogue using old tax-collection records. Another clue that this was the main synagogue: In accordance with Jewish traditions, it stubbornly faces east (toward Jerusalem), putting it at an angle at odds with surrounding structures. The sparse interior includes access to two small subterranean rooms with Roman walls topped by a medieval Catalan vault. Look through the glass floor to see dyeing vats used for a later shop on this site (run by former Jews who had been forcibly converted to Christianity).

▶ *At the synagogue, start back the way you came, continuing straight as the street becomes Carrer de la Fruita. At the T-intersection, turn left, then right, to find your way back to the martyrs monument. From here, turn right down Carrer del Bisbe to the...*

⓫ Carrer del Bisbe Bridge

This structure—reminiscent of Venice's Bridge of Sighs—connects the

Carrer del Bisbe has a Neo-Gothic look   Catalunya's autonomous seat of government

Catalan government building (on the right) with the Catalan president's ceremonial residence (on the left). Though the bridge looks medieval, it was constructed in the 1920s by Catalan architect Joan Rubió, who also did the carved ornamentation on the buildings.

It's a photographer's dream. Check out the jutting angels on the bridge, the basket-carrying maidens on the president's house, the gargoyle-like faces on the government building. Zoom in even closer. Find monsters, skulls, goddesses, old men with beards, climbing vines, and coats of arms—a Gothic museum in stone.

▶ Continue along Carrer del Bisbe to…

⑫ Plaça de Sant Jaume

This stately central square of the Barri Gòtic takes its name from the Church of St. James (in Catalan: Jaume, "jow-mah") that once stood here. Set at the intersection of ancient Barcino's main thoroughfares, this square was once a Roman forum. In that sense, it's been the seat of city government for 2,000 years. Today it's home to the two top governmental buildings in Catalunya: Palau de la Generalitat, and across from it, the Barcelona City Hall.

For more than six centuries, the **Palau de la Generalitat** (to your immediate right as you enter the square) has housed the offices of the autonomous government of Catalunya. It always flies the Catalan flag next to the obligatory Spanish one. Above the building's doorway is Catalunya's patron saint—St. George (Jordi), slaying the dragon. The dragon (which you'll see all over town) is an important Catalan symbol—both feared and respected, as is the bull in the rest of Spain. From these balconies, the nation's leaders (and soccer heroes) greet the people on momentous days.

The square is often the site of demonstrations, from a single aggrieved citizen with a megaphone to riotous thousands.

Facing the Generalitat across the square is the **Barcelona City Hall** (Casa de la Ciutat). It sports a statue (in the niche to the left of the door) of a different James—"Jaume el Conqueridor." The 13th-century King Jaume I is credited with freeing Barcelona from French control, granting self-government, and setting it on a course to become a major city. He was the driving force behind construction of the Royal Palace (which we'll see shortly).

Locals treasure the independence these two government buildings represent. Over the centuries, Catalunya has had to fight for its cultural and political identity. After thriving in the Middle Ages as an independent kingdom, the region fell under the control of the Spanish monarchs of Madrid. Then in the 20th century, Barcelona opposed the dictator Francisco Franco (who ruled from 1939 to 1975), and Franco retaliated. He abolished the regional government and (effectively) outlawed the Catalan language and customs. Two years after Franco's death, joyous citizens packed this square to celebrate the return of self-rule.

Look left and right down the main streets branching off the square; they're lined with ironwork streetlamps and balconies draped with plants. Carrer de Ferran, which leads to the Ramblas, is classic Barcelona.

In ancient Roman days, when Plaça de Sant Jaume was the town's central square, two main streets converged here—the Decumanus (Carrer del Bisbe) and the Cardus (Carrer de la Llibreteria/Carrer del Call). The forum's biggest building was a massive temple of Augustus, which we'll see next.

▶ *Facing the Generalitat, exit the square to the right of the building, heading uphill on tiny Carrer del Paradís. Follow this street as it turns right. When it swings left, pause at #10, the entrance to the...*

⑬ Roman Temple of Augustus

You're standing at the summit of Mont Tàber, the Barri Gòtic's highest spot. A plaque on the wall reads: "Mont Tàber, 16.9 meters" (elevation 55 feet). A millstone inlaid in the pavement at the doorstep of #10 also marks the spot. It was here that the ancient Romans founded the town of Barcino around 15 B.C. They built a *castrum* (fort) on the hilltop, protecting the harbor.

Go inside for a peek at the last vestiges of an imposing Roman

Impressive remains of a 2,000-year-old Roman temple that once stood facing Plaça Jaume

temple (Temple Roma d'August). All that's left now are four columns and some fragments of the transept and its plinth (good English info on-site). The huge columns, dating from the late first century B.C., are as old as Barcelona itself. They were part of the ancient town's biggest structure, a temple dedicated to the Emperor Augustus, who was worshipped as a god. These Corinthian columns (with deep fluting and topped with leafy capitals) were the back corner of a 120-foot-long temple that extended from here to Barcino's forum.

▶ *Continue down Carrer del Paridís one block. When you bump into the back end of the cathedral, take a right, and go downhill a block (down Carrer de la Pietat/Baixada de Santa Clara) until you emerge into a square called...*

⑭ Plaça del Rei

The buildings enclosing this square exemplify Barcelona's medieval past. The central section (topped by a five-story addition) was the core of the **Royal Palace** (Palau Reial Major). A vast hall on its ground floor once served as the throne room and reception room. From the 13th to the 15th century, the Royal Palace housed Barcelona's counts as well as the resident kings of Aragon. In 1493, a triumphant Christopher Columbus, accompanied by six New World natives (whom he called *"indios"*) and several pure-gold statues, entered the Royal Palace. King Ferdinand and Queen Isabella rose to welcome him home and honored him with the title "Admiral of the Oceans."

To the right is the palace's church, the 14th-century **Chapel of Saint Agatha,** which sits atop the foundations of a Roman wall. If the church is

Palace (center), Chapel (r), Viceroy (l)

Barcelona History Museum

hosting a temporary exhibit, you can see it for free (climb up the stairs and head inside).

To the left is the **Viceroy's Palace** (Palau del Lloctinent, for the ruler's right-hand man). This 16th-century building currently serves as the archives of the Crown of Aragon. After Catalunya became part of Spain in the 15th century, the Royal Palace became a small regional residence, and the Viceroy's Palace became the headquarters of the local Inquisition. Step inside to see the impressive Renaissance courtyard, a staircase with coffered wood ceilings, and a temporary exhibit space. Among the archive's treasures (though it's rarely on display) is the 1491 Santa Fe Capitulations, a contract between Columbus and the monarchs about his upcoming sea voyage. (See the poster of the yellowed document on the wall.)

Ironically, Columbus' discovery of new trade routes made Barcelona's port less important, and soon the royals moved elsewhere.

▶ *From the square, go around the corner onto Carrer del Veguer, where you'll find the entrance to the...*

⓯ Barcelona History Museum

This museum is a fine way to retrace all the history we've seen on this walk. You walk through the actual Roman foundations of Barcino (with exhibits that portray day-to-day life), enter a large hall and chapel from the city's medieval heyday, and see excavated objects from every period of Barcelona's history. (For details on the museum, ✪ see page 114).

▶ *Your walk is over. It's easy to get your bearings by backtracking to either Plaça de Sant Jaume or the cathedral. The Jaume I Metro stop is two blocks away (head downhill and turn left). From here, you're within striking distance of El Born (✪ see page 115), the Picasso Museum (✪ see page 117), or Barri Gòtic shopping (✪ see page 181). Or simply wander and enjoy Barcelona at its Gothic best.*

Cathedral of Barcelona Tour

Although Barcelona's cathedral doesn't rank among Europe's finest (and frankly, barely cracks the Top 20), it is important, easy to visit, and—much of the time—free to see. This quick tour introduces you to the cathedral's highlights: its vast nave, rich chapels, tomb of St. Eulàlia, and the oasis-like setting of the cloister. Other sights inside (which you'll pay separately for) are the elaborately carved choir, the elevator up to the view terrace, and the altarpiece museum.

ORIENTATION

Cost: Free in the morning (Mon-Sat before 12:45, Sun before 13:45) and late afternoon (after 17:15), but you have to pay for the cathedral's three minor sights—museum, view terrace, and choir (see "Other Cathedral Sights," below). Even though the church claims to be "closed" for several hours in the afternoon (Mon-Sat 13:00-17:00, Sun 14:00-17:00), you can still get in by paying €6 (which covers admission to the three interior sights). In other words, one way or another you'll pay around €6 to thoroughly tour the place; however, since the three extras inside are skippable, I'd aim to visit the church when it's free.

Hours: It's generally open to visitors Mon-Fri 8:00-19:30, Sat-Sun 8:00-20:00.

Getting There: The huge, can't-miss-it cathedral is in the center of the Barri Gòtic on Plaça de la Seu (Metro: Jaume I). To get here from Plaça de Catalunya, consider my ✪ Barri Gòtic Walk.

Getting In: The main, front door is open most of the time. While it can be crowded, the line generally moves fast. You can sometimes enter through the cloister around the side (through the door facing the martyrs monument on the small square along Carrer del Bisbe).

Information: Tel. 933-151-554, www.catedralbcn.org.

Length of This Tour: Allow 30 minutes, not counting the optional sights (choir, view terrace, museum).

Dress Code: The dress code is strictly enforced; don't wear tank tops, shorts, or skirts above the knee.

WCs: A tiny, semi-private WC is in the cloister.

Other Cathedral Sights: The three extra sights have separate fees (except during the afternoon church "closure," when €6 covers all three) and slightly shorter hours than the church itself: **Choir**—€2.50, Mon-Sat 9:00-19:00; **View Terrace**—€2.50, Mon-Sat 9:00-18:00, closed Sun; **Altarpiece Museum**—€2, daily 10:00-19:00, accessed from cloister. The extra sights can close even earlier on slow days.

Photography: Allowed without a flash.

Cathedral of Barcelona

N

20 Meters
20 Yards

↑ To Plaça de Catalunya
via Avinguda
Portal de l'Angel

Plaça Nova

To Plaça Maura, →
Santa Caterina Market
& El Born

◄ BARCINO SCULPTURE

ROMAN TOWERS

CASA D'ADRIACO

Plaça de la Seu

DIOCESÀ MUSEUM

CARRER DEL BISBE

CATHEDRAL MAIN ENTRANCE — STAIRS

SANTA LUCIA

❽ MUSEUM

FONT

CHRIST OF LEPANTO

❶ N A V E

S I D E

CLOISTER

GEESE

WC

❷

❷

C H A P E L S

CLOISTER ENTRANCE

❼

ST. RITA

ST. JORDI

POND

❸ CHOIR

C A R R E R   D E L S   C O M T E S

MONUMENT TO THE MARTYRS

C A T H E D R A L

To Plaça de Sant Jaume

CARRER DE LA PIETAT

CATALAN COAT OF ARMS

TRANSEPT

ELEV.

❺

❻

CLOISTER ENTRANCE

❹

HIGH ALTAR

To Roman Temple of Augustus

To Plaça del Rei

❶ Nave
❷ Side Chapels
❸ Choir
❹ High Altar
❺ To Crypt & Tomb of Eulàlia
❻ Elevator to Terrace
❼ Cloister
❽ Altarpiece Museum

THE TOUR BEGINS

This has been Barcelona's holiest spot for 2,000 years. The Romans built their Temple of Jupiter here. In A.D. 343, the pagan temple was replaced with a Christian cathedral. That building was supplanted by a Romanesque-style church (11th century). The current Gothic structure was started in 1298 and finished in 1450, during the glory days of the Catalan nation. The facade was humble, so in the 19th century the proud local bourgeoisie (enjoying a second golden age) redid it in an ornate, Neo-Gothic style. Construction was capped in 1913 with the central spire, 230 feet tall.

▶ *Enter the main door and take it all in.*

❶ The Nave

The spacious church is 300 feet long and 130 feet wide. Tall pillars made of stone blocks support the crisscross vaults. Each round keystone where the arches cross features a different saint. Typical of many Spanish churches, there's a choir—an enclosed area of wooden seats in the middle of the nave, creating a more intimate space for worship. The Gothic church

The cathedral, built in medieval times on an ancient site, features soaring arches in the nave

also has fine stained glass, ironwork chandeliers, a 16th-century organ (left transept), tombstones in the pavement, and an "ambulatory" floor plan, allowing worshippers to amble around to the chapel of their choice.

❷ Side Chapels

The nave is ringed with 28 chapels. Besides being worship spaces, these serve as interior buttresses supporting the roof (which is why the exterior walls are smooth, without the normal Gothic buttresses outside). Barcelona—the city of 32 official public holidays—honors many of the homegrown saints found in these chapels.

From the 13th to 15th century, these side chapels were moneymakers for the church—rented out to guilds to house their business offices. Notice how the iron gates are more than decorative—they also protected the goods and cash inside. The rich ornamentation was sponsored by local guilds as a kind of advertising, here in the community's most high-profile space.

The Church is still fundraising. The electronic candles that power your prayers cost €0.10 each. (A €0.50 coin lights five.)

▶ *Browse a few chapels, starting in the back-left corner of the nave (over your left shoulder as you enter the main door).*

The chapel at the back corner has an old **baptismal font** that once stood in the original fourth-century church. The Native Americans that Columbus brought to town were supposedly baptized here.

▶ *Work your way down the left aisle.*

The first chapel along the left wall is dedicated to **St. Severus,** the bishop here way back in A.D. 290.

The second chapel was by, for, and of the local **shoe guild.** Notice the two painted doors that lead to the back office. As the patron of shoe-makers was St. Mark, there are plenty of winged lions in this chapel.

▶ *Backtrack a bit, to the large chapel in the back-right corner.*

This chapel (reserved for worship) features the beloved **"Christ of Lepanto"** crucifix. They say the angular wooden figure of Christ leaned to dodge a cannonball during the history-changing Battle of Lepanto (1571), which stopped the Ottomans (and Islam) from advancing into Europe.

▶ *Now head down the right aisle.*

The second chapel has a statue of **St. Anthony** holding the Baby Jesus. His feast day (January 17) is one of many celebrated in the city with an appearance by the *gegants* (giant puppets), a street fair, horse races, and a blessing of pets.

The third chapel honors a 20th-century bishop who survived an assassination attempt in the cathedral cloister.

The golden fourth chapel is for **St. Roch** (at the top, pointing to his leg wound, above St. Pancraç), whose feast day is celebrated joyously in the Barri Gòtic in mid-August.

The fifth chapel has a black-and-white sideways statue of **St. Ramon (Raymond) of Penyafort** (1190-1275), the Dominican Bishop of Barcelona who heard Pope Gregory IX's sins and is the patron saint of lawyers (and, therefore, extremely busy). Ramon figures into the city's biggest festival, La Mercè, since he had a miraculous vision of the Virgin of Mercy.

The eighth chapel is worth a look for its over-the-top golden altarpiece decor nearly crowding out **Bishop Pacià**—considered one of the church fathers (c. A.D. 310-391).

▶ *If you want to visit the interior of the choir (described next), pay €2.50 or show your ticket at the choir entrance (straight ahead from the church's main doors). Otherwise, you can circle around to the far end and peer through the barrier.*

❸ Choir

The 15th-century choir *(coro)* features ornately carved stalls. During the standing parts of the Mass, the chairs were folded up, but VIPs still had those little wooden ledges to lean on. Each was creatively carved and—since you couldn't sit on sacred things—the artists were free to enjoy some secular and naughty fun here.

The choir, lined with carved wood stalls

Twin coffins of Cathedral benefactors

Beneath the high altar, stairs lead down to the tomb of the church's patron saint, Eulàlia

In 1518, the stalls were painted with the coats of arms of Europe's nobility. They gathered here as members of the Knights of the Golden Fleece to honor Charles V, King of Spain, who was making his first trip to the country he ruled. Find Charles' two-headed eagle, with the dangling lamb of the Golden Fleece. Next to Charles is the emblem (red and blue shield with lions and fleur-de-lis) of another invited guest, Henry VIII of England—who was a no-show. Check out the detail work on the impressive wood-carved pulpit near the altar, supported by flying angels.

▶ At the front of the church stands the...

❹ High Altar

Look behind the altar (beneath the crucifix) to find the archbishop's chair, or *cathedra*. As a cathedral, this church is the archbishop's seat—hence its Catalan nickname of *La Seu*. To the left of the altar are the organ and the elevator up to the terrace. To the right of the altar, the wall is decorated with Catalunya's yellow-and-red coat of arms. The two wooden coffins on the wall are of two powerful Counts of Barcelona (Ramon Berenguer I and his third wife, Almodis), who ordered the construction of the 11th-century Romanesque cathedral that preceded this structure.

▶ Descend the steps beneath the altar, into the crypt, to see the...

❺ Tomb of Eulàlia

The marble-and-alabaster sarcophagus (1327-1339) contains the remains of St. Eulàlia. The cathedral is dedicated to this saint. Thirteen-year-old Eulàlia, daughter of a prominent Barcelona family, was martyred by the Romans for her faith in A.D. 304. Murky legends say she was subjected to 13 tortures. First she was stripped naked and had her head shaved, though a miraculous snowfall hid her nakedness. Then she was rolled down the street in a barrel full of sharp objects. After further torments failed to kill her, she was crucified on an X-shaped cross—a symbol you'll find carved into pews and seen throughout the church.

The relief on the coffin's side tells her story in three episodes: She preaches Christianity to the pagan Roman ruler; he orders her to die (while she pleads for mercy); and she's crucified on the X-shaped cross. As one of Barcelona's patron saints, Eulàlia is honored with a festival (with *gegants*—giant puppets, fireworks, and human towers) in mid-February.

▶ The ❻ **elevator** in the left transept takes you up to the rooftop **terrace** for an expansive city view (€2.50).

Eulàlia's tomb, carved with her legends

Cloister geese—3 of the chosen 13

Otherwise, head to the right transept and go through the door to enter the...

❼ Cloister

Emerge into the circa-1450 cloister—an arcaded walkway surrounding a lush courtyard. Ahhhh. It's a tropical atmosphere of palm, orange, and magnolia trees; a fishpond; trickling fountains; and squawking geese.

From within the cloister, look back at the **arch** you just came through, an impressive mix of Romanesque (arches with chevrons, from the earlier church) and Gothic (pointy top).

The nearby **fountain** has a tiny statue of St. George slaying the dragon. George (Jordi in Spanish) is one of the patron saints of Catalunya and by far the most popular boy's name here. During the Corpus Christi festival in June, kids come here to watch a hollow egg dance atop the fountain's spray.

As you wander the cloister (clockwise), check out the **coats of arms** as well as the **tombs** in the pavement. These were rich merchants who paid good money to be buried as close to the altar as possible. Notice the symbols of their trades: scissors, shoes, bakers, and so on. After the church had sold out all its chapel space, they opened this cloister to donors. A second floor was planned (look up) but not finished.

The resident **geese** have been here for at least 500 years. There are always 13, in memory of Eulàlia's 13 years and 13 torments. Other legends say they're white as a symbol of her virginity. Before modern security systems, they acted as alarms, honking to alert the monk in charge. Faithful to tradition, they honk to this very day.

Farther along the cloister, next to the back door, the **Chapel of Santa**

Rita (patron saint of impossible causes) usually has the most candles. In the next corner of the cloister is the dark, barrel-vaulted **Chapel of Santa Lucía,** a small 13th-century remnant of the earlier Romanesque cathedral. People hoping for good eyesight (Santa Lucía's specialty) pray here. Notice the nice eyes in the modern restoration of the altar painting.

▶ *At the far end of the cloister, you'll find the...*

⑧ Altarpiece Museum (Museu Capitular)

The little museum (€2 entry) has the six-foot-tall 14th-century Great Monstrance, a ceremonial display case for the communion wafer. Made of gold and studded with jewels, it's really three separate parts: a church-like central section, topped by a crown canopy, standing on a golden chair. This huge monstrance with its wafer is paraded through the streets during the Corpus Christi festival. Nearby is a gold-plated silver statue of St. Eulàlia, carrying the X-shaped cross she was crucified on. An 11th-century baptismal font from the Romanesque church is also on view.

The next room, the Sala Capitular, has several altarpieces, including a *pietá* (a.k.a. *Desplà*) by Bartolomé Bermejo (1490). An anguished Mary cradles a twisted Christ against a bleak, stormy landscape. It's unique in Spanish art for its Italianesque, Renaissance 3-D. Rather than your basic gold backdrop, this has a strong foreground (the mourners), middle distance (the cross), and background (the city and distant hills). The kneeling donors who paid for the painting are photorealistic, complete with reading glasses and five o'clock shadows.

▶ *Our tour is over. May peace be with you.*

Picasso Museum Tour

Museu Picasso

This is the best collection in the country of the work of Spaniard Pablo Picasso (1881-1973). And, since Picasso spent his formative years (from the ages of 14 to 23) in Barcelona, it's the best collection of his early works anywhere. The museum is sparse on later, better-known works from his time of international celebrity; visit not to see famous canvases but to get an intimate portrait of the young man finding his way as an artist. By experiencing his youthful, realistic art, you can better understand his later, more challenging art and more fully appreciate his genius.

The artist himself donated pieces to the museum in his later life, happy to have a place showing off his work in the city of his youth.

ORIENTATION

Cost: €11, free all day first Sun of month and other Sun from 15:00.

Hours: Tue-Sun 10:00-19:50, closed Mon, last entry 20 minutes before closing.

Crowd-Beating Tips: There's almost always a line, sometimes with waits of more than an hour. The busiest times are mornings before 13:00, all day Tuesday, and during the free entry times on Sundays. If you have an Articket BCN (✪ see page 178), skip the line by going to the "Meeting Point" entrance (30 yards to the right of the main entrance). You can also skip the line by buying your ticket online at www.museupicasso.bcn.cat (no additional booking fee). Stuck in line without a ticket? Figure that about 25 people are admitted every 10 minutes.

Getting There: It's at Carrer de Montcada 15-23, in the colorful El Born neighborhood. From the Jaume I Metro stop, cross busy Via Laietana and head down Carrer de la Princesa, turning right on Carrer de Montcada. Or, for an interesting walk there from the cathedral, follow my El Born Walk (✪ see page 115).

Information: Tel. 932-563-000, www.museupicasso.bcn.cat.

Audioguide: The 1.5-hour audioguide (€3) is good.

Length of This Tour: Allow at least an hour.

Services: The ground floor, which is free to enter, has a required bag check, bookshop, WC, and cafeteria.

Photography: Strictly forbidden.

Cuisine Art: The museum has a good café (€8 sandwiches and salads). Near the museum, along Carrer de Montcada, are two recommended tapas bars: El Xampanyet and Bar del Pla.

Picasso Museum

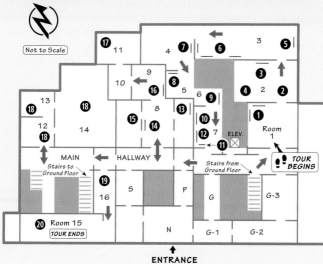

Not to Scale

MAIN **HALLWAY**

Stairs to Ground Floor

Stairs from Ground Floor

ELEV.

Room 1

👣 **TOUR BEGINS**

TOUR ENDS Room 15

ENTRANCE (AT GROUND LEVEL)

CARRER DE MONTCADA

← To Santa Caterina Market (5 min. walk)

To Church of Santa Maria del Mar (5 min. walk) →

To Jaume I Ⓜ (5 min. walk) & Cathedral (10 min. walk)

❶ Self-Portraits
❷ Portraits & Art-School Work
❸ First Communion
❹ Portrait of Artist's Mother
❺ Science and Charity
❻ Horta de San Joan
❼ Els Quatre Gats Menu Cover
❽ Velázquez Copy
❾ Cancan Dancer
❿ Still Life

⓫ Landscape
⓬ The Wait
⓭ The Forsaken
⓮ Rooftops of Barcelona
⓯ Portrait of Benedetta Bianco
⓰ Woman with Mantilla
⓱ Synthetic Cubism
⓲ Las Meninas Studies (3)
⓳ Ceramics
⓴ French Riviera

Rick Steves' | Pocket Barcelona

THE TOUR BEGINS

The Picasso Museum's collection of nearly 300 paintings is presented more or less chronologically. The art is scattered through several connected Gothic palaces. Be aware that specific pieces may be out for restoration or on tour, and the rooms are sometimes rearranged. But with the help of thoughtful English descriptions for each stage (and guards who don't let you stray), it's easy to follow the evolution of Picasso's life and work.

▶ Begin in rooms 1 and 2.

Boy Wonder

Pablo's earliest art is realistic and sober. The young genius gets serious about art at age 14, when his family moves to Barcelona and he enrolls in art school. Early **self-portraits** show the self-awareness of a blossoming intellect (and a kid who must have been a handful in junior high school). He seems proud—as if confident of future success.

Even at this young age, his **portraits** of grizzled peasants demonstrate surprising psychological insight and impressive technique. You'll see portraits of Pablo's first teacher, his father—himself a curator and artist who quit painting to nurture his young prodigy. Because his dedicated father kept everything his son ever did, Picasso must have the best-documented youth of any great painter.

Displays show Pablo's **art-school work.** Every time he starts breaking rules, he's sent back to the standard classic style. The assignment: Sketch nude models to capture human anatomy accurately.

▶ In room 2, you'll find more paintings relating to Pablo's...

Developing Talent

During a summer trip to Málaga in 1896, Picasso dabbles in a series of fresh, Impressionistic-style landscapes (relatively rare in Spain at the time). As a 15-year-old, Pablo dutifully enters art-school competitions. His first big work, **_First Communion_** (1896)—while portraying the prescribed religious subject—is more an excuse to paint his family. Notice his sister Lola's exquisitely painted veil. This piece is heavily influenced by the academic style of local painters.

Find the **portrait of his mother** (if it's on view—this fragile 1896 pastel is sometimes out for conservation). The teenage Pablo is working on the fine details and gradients of white in her blouse and the expression in her cameo-like face. Notice the signature. Spaniards keep both parents' surnames, with the father's first, followed by the mother's: Pablo Ruiz Picasso. Pablo is closer to his mom than his dad, and eventually he keeps just her name.

▶ *Continue into room 3.*

Early Success

Science and Charity (1897)*,* which won second prize at a fine-arts exhibition, got Picasso the chance to study in Madrid. Now Picasso conveys real feeling. The doctor (modeled on Pablo's father) represents science. The nun represents charity and religion. From her hopeless face and lifeless hand, it seems that Picasso believes nothing will save this woman from death. Pablo painted a little perspective trick: Walk back and forth across the room to see the bed stretch and shrink. Three small studies for this painting (on the right) show how this was an exploratory work. The frontier: light.

Picasso travels to Madrid for further study. Stifled by the stuffy

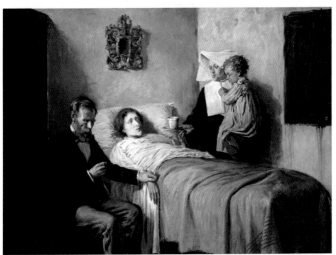

Science and Charity—The 16-year-old son of an art teacher wowed Spain with his mature insight

fine-arts school there, Pablo hangs out instead in the Prado Museum and learns by copying the masters. (An example of his impressive mimicry is coming up later, in Room 5.) Having absorbed the wisdom of the ages, in 1898 Pablo visits **Horta de San Joan,** a rural Catalan village, and finds his artistic independence. (See the small landscapes and scenes of village life he did there.) Poor and without a love in his life, he returns to Barcelona.

▶ *Head to room 4.*

Barcelona Freedom

Art Nouveau is all the rage in Barcelona when Pablo returns there in 1900. Upsetting his dad, he quits art school and falls in with the avant-garde crowd. These bohemians congregate daily at Els Quatre Gats ("The Four Cats," a popular restaurant to this day—✪ see page 40). Notice the **menu cover** he did for this favorite hangout. Further establishing his artistic freedom, he paints **portraits**—no longer of his family...but of his new friends (including one of Jaume Sabartés, who later became his personal assistant and donated the works to establish this museum). Only 19 years old, Pablo puts on his first one-man show.

▶ *Pause in the small room 5.*

Notice young Picasso's nearly perfect **copy** of a portrait of Philip IV by an earlier Spanish master, Diego Velázquez. (Near the end of this tour, we'll see a much older Picasso riffing on another Velázquez painting.)

▶ *The next few pieces are displayed in rooms 6 and 7.*

Paris

In 1900 Picasso makes his first trip to Paris, a city bursting with life, light, and love. Dropping the paternal surname Ruiz, Pablo establishes his commercial brand name: "Picasso." Here the explorer Picasso goes bohemian and befriends poets, prostitutes, and artists. He paints **cancan dancers** like Henri de Toulouse-Lautrec, **still lifes** like Paul Cézanne, brightly colored Fauvist works like Henri Matisse, and Impressionist **landscapes** like Claude Monet. In ***The Wait,*** the subject—with her bold outline and strong gaze—pops out from the Impressionistic background. It is Cézanne's technique of "building" a figure with "cubes" of paint that will inspire Picasso to invent Cubism—soon.

▶ *Turn right into the hall, then—farther along—right again, to find rooms 8 and 9.*

Picasso painted still lifes like Cezanne, later crystallizing the geometric shapes into Cubism

Blue Period

Picasso travels to Paris several times (he settles there permanently in 1904). The suicide of his best friend, his own poverty, and the influence of new ideas linking color and mood lead Picasso to his Blue Period (1901-1904). He cranks out stacks of blue art just to stay housed and fed. With blue backgrounds (the coldest color) and depressing subjects, this period was revolutionary in art history. Now the artist is painting not what he sees, but what he feels. Just off room 8, the touching 1903 portrait of a mother and child, **_The Forsaken,_** captures the period well. Painting misfits and street people, Picasso, like Velázquez and Toulouse-Lautrec, sees the beauty in ugliness. Back home in Barcelona, Picasso paints his hometown at night from **rooftops** (in the main part of room 8). The painting is still blue, but here we see proto-Cubism...five years before the first real Cubist painting.

▶ _Just off room 8, we get a hint of Picasso's..._

The Life of Pablo Picasso (1881-1973)

Pablo Picasso was the most famous and—OK, I'll say it—the greatest artist of the 20th century. Always exploring, he became the master of many styles (Cubism, Surrealism, Expressionism, and so on) and of many media (painting, sculpture, prints, ceramics, and assemblages). Still, he could make anything he touched look unmistakably like "a Picasso."

Born in Málaga, Spain, Picasso was the son of an art teacher. At a very young age, he quickly advanced beyond his teachers. Picasso's teenage works are stunningly realistic and capture the inner complexities of the people he painted. As a youth in Barcelona, he fell in with a bohemian crowd that mixed wine, women, and art.

In 1900, at age 19, Picasso started making trips to Paris. Four years later, he moved to the City of Light and absorbed the styles of many painters (especially Henri de Toulouse-Lautrec) while searching for his own artist's voice. His paintings of beggars and other social outcasts show the empathy of a man who was himself a poor, homesick foreigner. When his best friend, Spanish artist Carlos Casagemas, committed suicide, Picasso plunged into a **Blue Period** (1901-1904)—so called because the dominant color in these paintings matches their melancholy mood and subject matter (emaciated beggars, hard-eyed pimps, and so on).

In 1904, Picasso got a steady girl-friend (Fernande Olivier) and suddenly saw the world through rose-colored glasses—the **Rose Period.** He was further jolted out of his Blue Period by the "flat" look of the Fauves. Not satisfied with their take on 3-D, Picasso played with the "building blocks" of line and color to find new ways to reconstruct the real world on canvas. At his studio in Montmartre, Picasso and his neighbor Georges Braque worked together, in poverty so dire they often didn't know where their next bottle of wine was coming from.

And then, at the age of 25, Picasso reinvented painting. Fascinated by the primitive power of African and Iberian tribal masks, he sketched human faces with simple outlines and almond eyes. Intrigued by the body of his girlfriend, Fernande, he sketched it from every angle, then experimented with showing several different views on the same canvas. A hundred paintings and nine months later, Picasso gave birth to a monstrous canvas of five nude, fragmented prostitutes with mask-like faces—*Les Demoiselles d'Avignon* (1907). (The painting's name came not from the French city but from the once-brothel-lined Carrer d'Avinyo in Barcelona's Barri Gòtic.)

This bold new style was called **Cubism.** With Cubism, Picasso shattered the Old World and put it back together in a new way. The subjects are somewhat recognizable (with the help of the titles), but they're built with geometric shards (let's call them "cubes")—like viewing the world through a kaleidoscope of brown and gray. Cubism gives us several different angles of the subject at once—say, a woman seen from the front and side angles simultaneously, resulting in two eyes on the same side of the nose. This involves showing the traditional three dimensions, plus Einstein's new fourth dimension—the time it takes to walk around the subject to see other angles.

In 1918, Picasso married his first wife, Olga Kokhlova, with whom he had a son. He then traveled to Rome and entered a **Classical Period** (the 1920s) of more realistic, full-bodied women and children, inspired by the three-dimensional sturdiness of ancient statues. While he flirted with abstraction, throughout his life, Picasso always kept a grip on "reality." His favorite subject was people. The anatomy might be jumbled, but it's all there.

Though he lived in France and Italy, Picasso remained a Spaniard at heart, incorporating Spanish motifs into his work. Unrepentantly macho, he loved bullfights, seeing them as a metaphor for the timeless human interaction between the genders. The horse—clad with blinders

con't on next page

and pummeled by the bull—has nothing to do with the fight. To Picasso, the horse symbolizes the feminine, and the bull, the masculine. Spanish imagery—bulls, screaming horses, a Madonna—appears in Picasso's most famous work, *Guernica* (1937, on display in Madrid). The monumental canvas of a bombed village summed up the pain of Spain's brutal Civil War (1936-1939) and foreshadowed the onslaught of World War II.

At war's end, Picasso left Paris and his emotional baggage behind, finding fun in the sun in the **south of France** (1948-1954). Sun! Color! Water! Spacious skies! Freedom! Sixty-five-year-old Pablo Picasso was reborn, enjoying worldwide fame and the love of a beautiful 23-year-old painter named Françoise Gilot. Dressed in rolled-up white pants and a striped sailor's shirt, bursting with pent-up creativity, Picasso often cranked out more than one painting a day. Picasso's Riviera works set the tone for the rest of his life—sunny, lighthearted, uncomplicated, experimenting in new media and using motifs of the sea, of Greek mythology (fauns, centaurs), and animals (birds, goats, and pregnant baboons). His simple sketch of a dove holding an olive branch became an international symbol of peace.

Picasso also made collages, built "statues" out of wood, wire, ceramics, papier-mâché, or whatever, and even turned everyday household objects into statues (like his famous bull's head made of a bicycle seat with handlebar horns). **Multimedia** works like these have become so standard today that we forget how revolutionary they were when Picasso invented them. His last works have the playfulness of someone much younger. As it is often said of Picasso, "When he was a child, he painted like a man. When he was old, he painted like a child."

Rose Period

Picasso is finally lifted out of his funk after meeting a new lady, Fernande Olivier. He moves out of the blue and into the happier Rose Period (1904-1907). For a fine example, see the portrait of a woman wearing a classic Spanish mantilla **(Portrait of Benedetta Bianco).** Its glistening pink and reddish tones are the colors of flesh and sensuality. (This is the only actual Rose Period painting in the museum, but don't be surprised if it is out on loan.)

In **Woman with Mantilla** (room 9), we see a little Post-Impressionistic

Woman with Mantilla—Even after he moved to Paris, Picasso used motifs from his native land

Pointillism in a portrait that looks like a classical statue. Although it's a later work (from 1917), its cheery palette evokes the Rose Period.

▶ *Continue through room 10, into room 11.*

Cubism

Pablo's invention (roughly from 1906 to 1913, with fellow artist Georges Braque) of the shocking Cubist style is well known—at least I hope so, since this museum has no true Cubist paintings. The Cubist pulls apart the basic elements of a subject and re-presents them all at once from multiple viewpoints. In the museum, you'll see some so-called **Synthetic Cubist** paintings—a later variation that flattens the various angles, as opposed to the purer, original Analytical Cubist paintings, in which you can simultaneously see several 3-D facets of the subject.

▶ *Remember that this museum focuses on Picasso's early years, with very little from the decades between youthful Cubism and his sunset years on the French Riviera. Skip ahead more than 30 years and into rooms 12-14 (at the end of the main hallway, on the right).*

Picasso and Velázquez

This series of rooms relates to what many consider the greatest painting by anyone, ever: Diego Velázquez's *Las Meninas* (the 17th-century original is displayed in Madrid's Prado Museum). Heralded as the first completely realistic painting, *Las Meninas* became an obsession for Picasso centuries later.

Picasso, who had great respect for Velázquez, painted more than **40 interpretations** of this piece. Picasso seems to enjoy a relationship of equals with Velázquez. Like artistic soul mates, the two Spanish geniuses spar and tease. Picasso deconstructs Velázquez and then injects light, color, and perspective as he improvises on the earlier masterpiece. In Picasso's big black-and-white canvas, the king and queen (reflected in the mirror in the back of the room) are hardly seen, while the painter towers above everyone. The two women of the court on the right look like they're in a tomb—but they're wearing party shoes. Browse the various studies, a playground of color and perspective. See the fun Picasso had playing paddleball with Velázquez's tour de force—filtering Velázquez's realism through the kaleidoscope of Cubism.

▶ *Head back into the* **ceramics** *area (room 16), where you'll find a flock of carefree white birds, and continue into room 15.*

Synthetic Cubism

Picasso improvised off the master Velázquez

The French Riviera

Picasso spends the last 36 years of his life living simply in the south of France. He said many times that "Paintings are like windows open to the world." We see his sunny Riviera world: With simple black outlines and Crayola colors, Picasso paints sun-splashed nature, peaceful doves, and the joys of the beach. He dabbles in the timeless art of ceramics, shaping bowls and vases into fun animals decorated with simple, childlike designs. He now has little kids of his own and hangs out with uncomplicated (even childlike) artists like Marc Chagall.

Picasso died with brush in hand, still growing. Sadly, since Picasso vowed never to set foot in a fascist, Franco-ruled Spain, the artist never returned to his homeland...and never saw this museum. However, to the end, Picasso continued exploring and loving life through his art.

▶ *Our tour is finished. You're in the heart of the delightful El Born neighborhood. For a self-guided walk of this area,* ✪ *see my El Born Walk on page 115.*

Eixample Walk

From Plaça de Catalunya to Casa Milà (and Beyond)

Literally "The Expansion," L'Eixample is where Barcelona spread when it burst at the seams in the 19th century. City planners created a refreshingly open grid plan of broad, straight boulevards—the opposite of the claustrophobic Gothic lanes that had contained locals for centuries.

In the mid-1800s, Barcelona was humming. The Eixample reflects two important historic movements: the revival of Catalan cultural pride (the Renaixença), and the emergence of Catalunya's own spin on Art Nouveau (Modernisme). It was a perfect storm of urban planning, architectural innovation, Industrial Age technology, ample wealth, and Catalan pride.

The core of this walk is two of the city's Modernista musts—the Block of Discord and Casa Milà. We'll also wind through some untouristy residential neighborhoods that showcase the vibrant vibe of Barcelona today.

ORIENTATION

Length of This Walk: Allow 1.5 hours—more if you tour Casa Milà or Casa Batlló. With less time, focus on the Block of Discord and Casa Milà.

Reservations: If you want to see the interiors, reservations are smart at both Casa Milà and Casa Batlló.

Getting There: This walk starts at Plaça de Catalunya (Metro: Plaça de Catalunya).

When to Go: By day, you can visit the interiors of Casa Milà, Casa Batlló, the Church of the Holy Conception (closes for mid-afternoon siesta), the Fundació Antoni Tàpies, and La Concepció Market (Tue-Fri 8:00-20:00, Mon and Sat 8:00-15:00, closed Sun). At night, the interiors are closed, but you can still see many floodlit facades and enjoy the lively tapas bar scene.

Casa Batlló: €18.15, daily 9:00-20:00; for ticket info, ✪ see page 120.

Casa Milà: €15, daily March-Oct 9:00-20:00, Nov-Feb 9:00-18:30, last entry 30 minutes before closing, for reservation info and crowd-beating tips, ✪ see page 121.

Eating: Several fine tapas bars and restaurants are on or near the course of this walk. For details, ✪ see page 160.

Background

Barcelona boomed in the 1800s, with its population doubling (from a half-million to a million) over the course of one century.

Before its upsurge, Barcelona languished through centuries of stagnation: Columbus' discoveries had shifted trade from the Mediterranean

to the Atlantic. Catalunya also suffered under the thumb of Madrid, which feared—perhaps rightfully—a Catalan uprising.

Eventually Barcelona was allowed to trade with the Americas, bringing new wealth. And locally, this land of abundant coal deposits and many rivers flowing from the Pyrenees to the Mediterranean provided the perfect resources for powering textile mills. Industrialization attracted tens of thousands of workers from all over Spain. Barcelona was back on the map.

But the upwardly mobile city had nowhere to grow. Because of the Madrid government's centuries-old restrictions, the city was forced to stay within its medieval walls. By the mid-19th century, 200,000 residents were crammed into the Old City. It was a grimy, soot-covered slum, where disease was rampant and the quality of life was miserable. It was clear that expansion was necessary. (At around the same time, Paris, Vienna, Copenhagen, and other cities were dealing with similar growing pains.)

Finally, in 1854, Queen Isabella II loosened Madrid's grip on Barcelona. She allowed the growing city to tear down the medieval wall and expand northward. Because very little existed outside the Old City, urban planners had a blank slate.

Civil engineer Ildefons Cerdà (1815-1876) created a remarkably modern and efficient grid of streets, but with a people-friendly twist: By snipping off the building corners, light and spacious octagonal "squares" were created at every intersection. Each block was to have easy access to its own hospital, park, market, schools, and day-care centers. Strict zoning codes made sure sunlight would reach every unit. The hollow space inside each "block" of apartments would form a neighborhood park. The Eixample was a modern marvel of urban planning.

Rich-and-artsy big shots gobbled up this prime real estate, especially along the main drag, Passeig de Gràcia. They built mansions to show off their wealth and status, hiring the best and brightest architects in the business (✪ see the sidebar on page 86).

Today's Eixample is still the city's most desirable neighborhood. The heart of the Eixample is the Quadrat d'Or, or "Golden Quarter," with the richest collection of Modernista facades...and the richest local residents. It's also one center of the local gay community (especially around Carrer d'Aribau), earning it the nickname "Gayshample."

Eixample Walk

Modernisme and the Renaixença

Modernisme is Barcelona's unique contribution to the Europe-wide Art Nouveau movement. Meaning "a taste for what is modern"—things like streetcars, electric lights, and big-wheeled bicycles—this free-flowing organic style lasted from 1888 to 1906.

The starting point for the style was a kind of Neo-Gothic, clearly inspired by medieval castles, towers, and symbols—logically, since architects wanted to recall Barcelona's glory days of the 1400s when it ruled a shipping empire. From the Neo-Gothic look, Antoni Gaudí branched off on his own, adding the color and curves we most associate with Barcelona's Modernisme look.

The aim was to create objects that were both practical and decorative. Modernista architects experimented with new construction techniques, especially concrete, which they could use to make a hard stone building that curved and rippled like a wave. Then they sprinkled it with brightly colored glass and tile. The structure was fully modern, but the decoration was a clip-art collage of nature images, exotic Moorish or Chinese themes, and fanciful Gothic crosses and knights to celebrate Catalunya's medieval glory days.

It's ironic to think that Modernisme was a response to the Industrial Age—and that all those organic shapes were only made possible thanks to Eiffel Tower-like iron frames. The Eixample's fanciful facades and colorful, leafy ornamentation were built at the same time as the first skyscrapers in Chicago and New York City.

Fueling Modernisme was the Catalan cultural revival movement called the Renaixença. As Europe was waking up to the modern age, downtrodden peoples across Europe—from the Basques to the Irish to the Hungarians to the Finns—were throwing off the cultural domination of other nations and celebrating what made their own cultures unique. Here in Catalunya, the Renaixença encouraged everyday people to get excited about all things Catalan—from their language, patriotic dances, and inspirational art to their surprising style of architecture.

THE WALK BEGINS

▶ *Begin at Plaça de Catalunya. Head up the broad boulevard (Passeig de Gràcia) at the top end of the giant El Corte Inglés department store. Walk up one block (on the right side of this street) to the huge intersection with Gran Via de les Corts Catalanes; there's a big fountain in the middle.*

① Passeig de Gràcia

In the 500 feet between here and the Barri Gòtic, you've traveled 500 years—from the medieval Gothic vibe of the Barri Gòtic to the ambitiously modern late-19th-century Eixample.

In Catalan, *passeig* means "boulevard"—and this one leads to Gràcia, once a separate town but now a neighborhood in Barcelona. Glancing at a map, you'll see that this street angles slightly through the otherwise uniform grid. It was prime real estate. Barcelona's richest built their mansions here, as close as possible to Placa de Catalunya. (One of the few surviving mansions, now the Comedia theater, is kitty-corner across the intersection—just beyond the fountain.) To this day, it's the top street in

Plaça de Catalunya—dividing old and new Barcelona—marks the start of stately Passeig de Gràcia

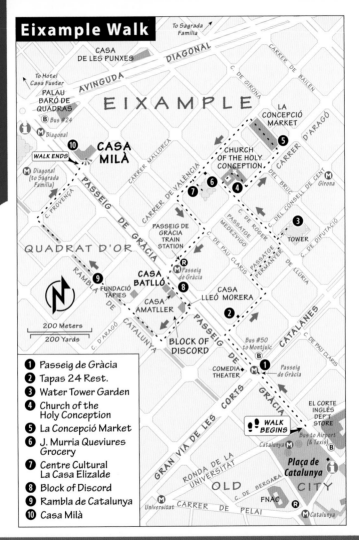

Eixample Walk

To Sagrada Familia

CASA DE LES PUNXES

DIAGONAL

CARRER DE BAILEN

To Hotel Casa Fuster

AVINGUDA

C. DE GIRONA

PALAU BARÓ DE QUADRAS

B Bus #24

M Diagonal

EIXAMPLE

LA CONCEPCIÓ MARKET

CASA MILÀ ⑩

CARRER D'ARAGÓ

CHURCH OF THE HOLY CONCEPTION

WALK ENDS

CARRER MALLORCA

⑤

M Diagonal (to Sagrada Familia)

PASSEIG DE GRÀCIA

CARRER DE VALÈNCIA

⑥

④

DEL BRUC

C. DEL CONSELL DE CENT

Girona

⑦

PASSATGE MEDEZVIGO

C. DE ROGER

QUADRAT D'OR

PASSEIG DE GRÀCIA TRAIN STATION

PASSATGE PERMANYER

TOWER ③

C. DE LLÚRIA

C. DE DIPUTACIÓ

N

C. PROVENÇA

RAMBLA DE CATALUNYA

FUNDACIÓ TÀPIES

⑨

CASA BATLLÓ

M Passeig de Gràcia

R

C. DE PAU CLARIS

⑧

CASA LLEÓ MORERA

CASA AMATLLER

CARRER D'ARAGÓ

200 Meters

200 Yards

BLOCK OF DISCORD

②

PASSEIG DE GRÀCIA

CATALANES

C. DE PAU CLARIS

Bus #50 to Montjuïc

B

Passeig de Gràcia

M

① **Passeig de Gràcia**
② **Tapas 24 Rest.**
③ **Water Tower Garden**
④ **Church of the Holy Conception**
⑤ **La Concepció Market**
⑥ **J. Murria Queviures Grocery**
⑦ **Centre Cultural La Casa Elizalde**
⑧ **Block of Discord**
⑨ **Rambla de Catalunya**
⑩ **Casa Milà**

COMEDIA THEATER

GRAN VIA DE LES CORTS

WALK BEGINS

Bus to Airport (& Taxis) **B**

EL CORTE INGLÉS DEP'T STORE

Catalunya **M**

RONDA DE LA UNIVERSITAT

OLD

CITY

Plaça de Catalunya

Universitat **M**

CARRER DE PELAI

C. DE BERGARA

FNAC

R

M Catalunya

town. Notice the extra-wide girth, the inviting park-like median strips, and the unique Modernista lampposts anchored by Gaudí-style benches slathered with broken white tile mosaics.

Despite their varied facades, most Eixample homes share an identical design. Shops and businesses inhabit the ground floor. Above that is a taller first (our "second") floor. This was the *piano nobile,* where the wealthy family lived. It's usually more elaborate than the other floors, with balconies or bay windows. It's no accident that Modernista mansions have big bay windows and outlandish decoration: The wealthy wanted to see and be seen, and to be recognized for their forward-thinking embrace of the new art. Higher up, the smaller floors hold less spacious apartments (though after the elevator was invented, penthouse living became popular). Many houses have two doors—one for the owners, and another for the upstairs tenants. Most house blocks had an interior garden courtyard for ventilation and light, although over time many have been covered over by one-story structures or parking lots.

Because the Eixample was developed during the Renaixença, you'll spot Catalan themes, such as St. George (Jordi)—the local patron saint—slaying the dragon. You might see the Catalunyan flag, with its red-and-gold stripes, or the flag of St. George (a red cross on a white field). Speaking of Catalan pride, this street is where massive crowds of Catalans sometimes gather to demonstrate for Catalunyan autonomy. "*Som una nació,*" they chant. "*Nosaltres decidim.*" We are a nation. We decide.

Continue to the intersection with Carrer de la Diputació. With its four corners cropped off, the intersection becomes a wide-open, pleasant space for café tables, inviting benches, or public art.

▶ *From here, you could continue directly to the Block of Discord. But, to see a different side to the neighborhood, turn right on Carrer de la Diputació.*

❷ Tapas 24

A few steps down on the left is a great example of the many trendy Eixample tapas bars (for more listings, ✪ see page 160). It's run by a disciple of Catalunya's most famous chef, Ferran Adrià, who put Catalunya on the gastronomic map with his trendsetting techniques. Adrià's trademark dish is a "liquid olive," which looks like a real olive but is actually a thin spherical membrane filled with intensely flavored essence of olive. Foodies now flock to Barcelona to sample the work of Adrià's apprentices, including chef Carles Abellan of Tapas 24.

Continue one block down Carrer de la Diputació, noticing the typical tile paving stones (four squares with a circle in each one), which have become a symbol of Barcelona.

▶ *At the corner, turn left up Carrer de Pau Claris. Halfway up the block, turn right into the gated **passage** (Passatge Permanyer, at #116). Popping out the other end, cross the street and jog 30 yards to the left, then go down the passage at #56 (on the right, marked Jardins de Torre de les Aigües, open daily 10:00-sunset). This leads you to a...*

❸ Water Tower Garden

This tranquil (if somewhat sterile) courtyard has trees, benches, and a pool, all watched over by a brick water tower from 1867. In the summer, a temporary "beach" is sometimes created here. In the original vision of the Eixample, each block was supposed to have a shared central courtyard like this. But over time, many were converted to buildings or parking lots. More recently, the city of Barcelona has slowly begun restoring Cerdà's original public spaces.

▶ *Exiting the garden the way you entered, turn right and head up Carrer de Roger de Llúria. Cross Carrer del Consell de Cent (passing under a pretty yellow façade).*

   Continue another block and cross another street (Carrer d'Aragó). Go straight a half-block, entering the cloister at #70 (on the right), entering the...

❹ Church of the Holy Conception

Work your way through the cloister to the interior of the church. This 13th-century Gothic church once stood in the Old City. But in the 1870s, it was moved, brick by brick, to this spot, to bring a bit of old-time religion to the newly developed Eixample. The bell tower came from a different Gothic church.

▶ *Exiting the church through its front door, turn left and continue one block. On the left is...*

❺ La Concepció Market

Though just as colorful as La Boqueria (on the Ramblas) and the Santa Caterina Market (in El Born), this market has virtually zero tourists. Walk through the building, from one end to the other. It's a good place to sample

Water Tower Garden's brick tower once provided Eixample residents with running water

The Stars of Modernisme

Yes, you'll hear plenty about Gaudí, but he's merely one of many great minds who contributed to the architectural revolution of Modernisme. Here's a rundown of the movement's major players.

Antoni Gaudí (1852-1926), Barcelona's most famous Modernista artist, was descended from four generations of metalworkers—a lineage of which he was quite proud. He incorporated ironwork into his architecture and came up with novel approaches to architectural structure and space. Gaudí's work strongly influenced his younger Catalan contemporary, Salvador Dalí. Notice the similarities: While Dalí was creating unlikely and shocking juxtapositions of photorealistic images, Gaudí did the same in architecture—using the spine of a reptile for a bannister or a turtle shell  design on windows. Entire trips (and lives) are dedicated to seeing the works of Gaudí, but on a brief visit in Barcelona, the ones most worth considering are his great unfinished church, the Sagrada Família; several mansions in the town center, including Casa Milà, Casa Batlló, and Palau Güell; and Park Güell, his ambitious and never-completed housing development.

Lluís Domènech i Montaner (1850-1923), a professor and politician, was responsible for some major civic buildings, including his masterwork, the Palace of Catalan Music (✪ described on page 114). He also designed Casa Lleó Morera on the Block of Discord (described later) and Casa Fuster (now a luxury hotel—✪ see page 91). Although

local cheeses, buy olives, or pick up some fruit. At the far end, you'll emerge into a delightful flower market crowding the sidewalk.

▶ *Turn left and walk along...*

Carrer de València

Stroll a few blocks and enjoy some features of everyday life in the Eixample. You'll pass flower stands, the turreted Municipal Conservatory (a music

Gaudí is more famous, Domènech i Montaner's work is perhaps more purely representative of the Modernista style.

Josep Puig i Cadafalch (1867-1956) was a city planner who oversaw the opening up of Via Laietana through the middle of the Old City. He was instrumental in the redevelopment of Montjuïc for the 1929 World Expo. As a home-builder, he designed Casa de les Punxes (✪ see page 91) and Casa Amatller on the Block of Discord (described later). He designed a brick factory that has recently been transformed into the cutting-edge CaixaForum exhibition space (✪ see page 128). Perhaps most importantly, Puig i Cadafalch designed the building housing Els Quatre Gats (✪ see page 156), a bar that became a cradle of sorts for the whole Modernista movement.

All architects worked with a team of people who, while not famous, made real contributions. For example, Gaudí's colleague **Josep Maria Jujol** (1879-1949) is primarily responsible for much of what Gaudí became known for—the broken-tile mosaic decorations (called *trencadís*) on Park Güell's benches and Casa Milà's chimneys.

Though not an artist, businessman **Eusebi Güell** (1846-1918) is worth a mention. He used his nearly $90 billion fortune to bankroll Gaudí and others, much as the Medici financed Michelangelo and Leonardo da Vinci. Güell's name still adorns two of Gaudí's most important works: Palau Güell and Park Güell (✪ described on pages 110 and 130).

school), an ugly brick monstrosity, and (at #293) a fine Modernista building with wrought-iron railings and twin bay windows. Peek inside ❻ **J. Murria Queviures** (at Carrer de Roger de Llúria 85), a classic old-fashioned gourmet deli. The vintage ad on the corner—dubbed *La Mona y el Mono (The Classy Lady and the Monkey)*—advertised anise liquor to Modernista-era clients.

Explore the ❼ **Centre Cultural La Casa Elizalde** (at Carrer de

València 302), a hive of city-sponsored classes and activities. Heading down the hall, you'll pop out into an appealing park in the middle of the block with benches and WCs. At Carrer de València 300, the Multiplastic shop sells all manner of sleek, colorful Euro-housewares.

Ponder the fact that in just a few blocks, we've passed a church, a market, a school, a community center, and an array of shops. This is very much in keeping with the original vision for the Eixample: a series of self-sufficient neighborhoods that give residents easy access to the things they need.

▸ *At the end of the block, go left down Carrer de Pau Claris. After a block, turn right on the wide Carrer d'Aragó. Walk one block, and you'll find yourself kitty-corner from the...*

❽ Block of Discord (Illa de la Discòrdia)

One block, three buildings, three astonishingly creative Modernista architects. Over a short span of time, the three big names of Catalunya's bold Art Nouveau architectural movement erected innovative facades along this one short stretch of Passeig de Gràcia. Although each of these architects has better works elsewhere in town, this is the most convenient place to see their sharply contrasting visions side by side. Besides these three famous buildings, the whole block is a jumble of delightful architectural whimsy. Reliefs, coats of arms, ironwork, gables, and bay windows adorn otherwise ordinary buildings.

▸ *Work your way down the block, beginning with the unmistakably Gaudí-style facade that's one building in from the corner.*

Casa Batlló (#43)

First and most famous is the green-blue ceramic-speckled facade of Casa Batlló, designed by Antoni Gaudí (you can tour the interior—❸ see listing on page 120). It has tibia-like pillars and skull-like balconies, inspired by the time-tested natural forms that Gaudí knew made the best structural supports. The tiled roof has a soft-ice-cream-cone turret topped with a cross. It's thought that Gaudí based the work on the popular legend of St. George *(Jordi)* slaying the dragon: The humpback roofline suggests a cresting dragon's back, and the smallest, top balcony is shaped like a rosebud (echoing the legend that a rose grew in the place where St. George spilled the dragon's blood). But some see instead a Mardi Gras theme, with mask-like balconies, a facade flecked with purple and gold

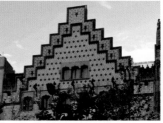

Gaudí's dragon-spine roof on Casa Batlló   Casa Amatller's step-gable roofline

confetti, and the ridge of a harlequin's hat up top. The inscrutable Gaudí preferred to leave his designs open to interpretation.

▶ Next door is...

Casa Amatller (#41)

Josep Puig i Cadafalch completely remodeled this house for the Amatller family. The facade features a creative mix of three of Spain's historical traditions: Moorish-style pentagram-and-vine designs; Gothic-style tracery, gargoyles, and bay windows; and the step-gable roof from Spain's Habsburg connection to the Low Countries. Notice the many layers of the letter "A": The house itself (with its gable) forms an A, as does the decorative frieze over the bay window on the right side of the facade. Within that frieze, you'll see several more "As" sprouting from branches (*amatller* means "almond tree"). The reliefs above the smaller windows show off the hobbies of the Amatller clan: Find the cherubs holding the early box camera, the open book, and the amphora jug (which the family collected). Look through the second-floor bay window to see the corkscrew column. If you want, you can pop inside for a closer look at the elaborate entrance hall.

For another dimension of Modernisme, peek into the ground-floor windows of the Bagues Joieria jewelry shop and notice the slinky pieces by Spanish Art Nouveau jeweler Masriera.

▶ Now head left, to the end of the block. There, on the corner, you'll find...

Casa Lleó Morera (#35)

Here's another paella-like mix of styles, this one by the architect Lluís Domènech i Montaner, who also designed the Palace of Catalan Music (you'll notice similarities). The lower floors have classical columns and a

Greek-temple-like bay window. Farther up are Gothic balconies of rosettes and tracery, while the upper part has faux Moorish stucco work. The whole thing is ornamented with fantastic griffins, angels, and fish. Flanking the third-story windows are figures holding the exciting inventions of the day—the camera, light bulb, and gramophone—designed to demonstrate just how modern the homeowners were in this age of Modernisme. Unfortunately, the wonderful interior is closed to the public.

▶ *From here, it's several long blocks gently uphill to Gaudí's Modernista masterpiece, Casa Milà. While the easiest route is to simply turn around and plow back up Passeig de Gràcia—passing top-end shops—you may find it more interesting to detour around the block to...*

❾ Rambla de Catalunya

As you head up Rambla de Catalunya, you'll find a narrower, more manageable street with a delightful, park-like median strip. It's lined by inviting cafés and shops—boutiques that are still upscale, but generally more local and unique than those on the main drag.

On the way up, a half-block detour (to the right) on Carrer d'Aragó gets you to the **Fundació Antoni Tàpies,** dedicated to the 20th-century abstract artist from Barcelona. The Montaner-designed building sums up the Modernist credo: modern brick, iron, and glass materials; playful decorative motifs; and a spacious, functional, and light-filled interior. It's pricey to enter (€7), but fans will enjoy Tàpies' distinct mud-caked canvases. Tàpies (1923-2012) laid the canvas on the floor, covered it with wet varnish, and sprinkled in dust, dirt, and paint. Then he drew simple designs in the

Hometown boy Tàpies' modern art museum

Casa Milà—Gaudí's icon of Modernisme

still-wet goop, capturing the primitive power of cavemen tracing the first art in mud with a stick.

▶ *When you get to Carrer de Provença, turn right and make your way to...*

⑩ Casa Milà (a.k.a. La Pedrera)

This Gaudí exterior laughs down on the crowds filling Passeig de Gràcia. Casa Milà, also called La Pedrera ("The Quarry"), has a much-photographed roller coaster of melting-ice-cream eaves. This is Barcelona's quintessential Modernista building and was Gaudí's last major work (1906-1910) before he dedicated his final years to the Sagrada Família.

The building has a steel structural skeleton to support its weight (a new construction technique at the time). Gaudí's planned statues of the Virgin Mary and archangels were vetoed by the owner. If you have time— and the line's not too long—consider touring the house's interior and rooftop, or just take a peek inside the main atrium for free. (✪ For more about the interior, see page 121).

▶ *Our walk is over. From here, you can head back to Plaça de Catalunya— it's a straight shot, seven blocks down Passeig de Gràcia. The Diagonal Metro station near Casa Milà, on the L3 (green) line, has easy connections to Plaça de Catalunya and other key stops.*

But for those with a little more energy, consider exploring some sights...

Nearby

A few steps up Passeig de Gràcia from Casa Milà, the fun **Vinçon** shop has stylish office and home furnishings. Two blocks farther up you run into **Avinguda Diagonal,** the aptly named boulevard that slashes diagonally through the Eixample grid. Two buildings along Diagonal were designed by Josep Puig i Cadafalch: the plateresque **Palau Baró de Quadras** (Diagonal 373), which is now a cultural center that's free to enter; and the distinctively turreted **Casa de les Punxes** ("House of Spikes," at #416).

If you continue north across Diagonal, you enter **Gràcia,** a neighborhood with a small town feel, narrower streets, and a youthful student scene. There you'll find **Hotel Casa Fuster** (Passeig de Gràcia 132), a fine Modernista building by Lluís Domènech i Montaner that hosts jazz at night (✪ see page 183) and was featured in Woody Allen's film *Vicky Cristina Barcelona.*

A great place to end your explorations is back at the intersection of Passeig de Gràcia and Diagonal, where you'll find the Catalunya TI (at Passeig de Gràcia 107). Enter through the gate to the left of the TI entrance to discover an enjoyable little **park**—a tropical oasis in the heart of the city.

▶ *From the intersection of Passeig de Gràcia and Diagonal, you have several transportation options:*

*The handy **L3 (green) Metro** leaves from the Diagonal Metro stop, going to Plaça de Catalunya, Liceu (middle of the Ramblas), and Drassanes (bottom of the Ramblas).*

*The **L5 (blue) Metro** (enter the Diagonal Metro one block west on Carrer del Rosselló) goes to Sagrada Família.*

***Bus #24** goes to Gaudí's Park Güell. Catch it on Passeig de Gràcia just south of Diagonal, same side of street as Casa Milà; get off at the Carretera Carmel-Parc Güell stop.*

Sagrada Família Tour

Architect Antoni Gaudí's most famous and awe-inspiring work is this un-finished, super-sized church. With its cake-in-the-rain facade and other-worldly spires, the church is an icon of Barcelona and its trademark Modernista style. As an architect, Gaudí's foundations were classics, na-ture, and religion. The church represents all three.

Nearly a century after his death, people continue to toil to bring Gaudí's designs to life. There's something powerful about a community of committed people with a vision, working on a church that won't be finished in their lifetime—as was standard in the Gothic age. It's a testament to the generations of architects, sculptors, stonecutters, and donors who've been caught up in the audacity of Gaudí's astonishing vision. If there's any building on earth I'd like to see, it's the Sagrada Família...finished.

ORIENTATION

Cost: €13 (cash only). Part of your admission funds the ongoing work.

Hours: Daily April-Sept 9:00-20:30, Oct-March 9:00-18:30, last entry 30 minutes before closing.

Advance Reservations: To avoid the ticket-buying line (with waits up to 45 minutes), you can reserve an entry time and buy tickets in advance at www.sagradafamilia.cat (€1.30 booking fee). With your pre-purchased ticket, you get immediate entry at the "online ticket office" window.

Alternatively, you can get tickets from ATMs at many La Caixa bank branches throughout the city—including the branch to the left as you face the ticket windows and Passion Facade (at the corner, just across the street). If tickets are available, you can buy them for the same day, even for immediate entry. However, not every La Caixa ATM sells tickets (use their larger ServiCaixa machines), and the instructions may be in Spanish (though English-only users can figure it out). Start the transaction by selecting "Event Tickets/Entradas Espectáculos" at the top of the screen.

Crowd-Beating Tips: Lines are longest in mid-morning, so arrive right at 9:00 (when the church opens) or after 16:00. To skip the line, buy advance tickets, take a tour, or hire a private guide.

Getting There: It's located at Carrer de Mallorca 104 at the far edge of the Eixample neighborhood. From the Sagrada Família Metro stop, exit toward Plaça de la Sagrada Família. The entrance and ticket windows are at the west end of the church (the Passion Facade).

Information: Tel. 932-073-031, www.sagradafamilia.cat.

Tours: English-language tours (€4, 50 minutes) run daily at 11:00 and 13:00, and sometimes at 12:00. Good 1.5-hour audioguide-€4.

Elevators: Two different elevators (€3 each, pay at main ticket office, each ticket comes with an entry time) take you partway up the towers for a great view of the city and church. The easier option is the Passion Facade elevator (no walking required). The Nativity Facade elevator lets you cross the dizzying bridge between the towers, but you'll need to take the stairs down.

Length of This Tour: Allow 1.5 hours.

Background—A Dream Made Real

For over 130 years, Barcelona has labored to bring Antoni Gaudí's vision to reality. In 1883, Gaudí signed up for the fledgling project, imagining a Gothic-style church with his own Art Nouveau/Modernisme touches. He labored on the Sagrada Família for 43 years. At his death (1926), the church was about 20 percent complete. Since then, construction has moved forward in fits and starts. Like Gothic churches of medieval times, the design has evolved over the decades.

The Spanish Civil War (1936-39) halted all work. In the 1950s, building resumed, though slowly. The pace picked up considerably with the advent of computer technology (1980s) and the energy of the '92 Olympics. By 2010, the roof was finished, in time for Pope Benedict XVI to dedicate the church as a basilica.

Today it's still a work in progress, with a long way to go. The site bristles with cranking cranes, rusty forests of rebar, and scaffolding. The present architect has been at it since 1985. The work is funded exclusively by private donations and entry fees. There is visible progress, year after year. As I stepped inside on my last visit, the brilliance of Gaudí's vision for the interior was apparent.

Tentative plans are that the church will be finished in 2026, for the 100th anniversary of Gaudí's death. Make a date to attend the dedication ceremonies with your kids or grandkids...to teach them a lesson in delayed gratification.

THE TOUR BEGINS

► *Start at the ticket entrance (at the Passion Facade) on the western side of the church. The view is best from the park across the street. Before heading to the ticket booth, take in the...*

❶ Exterior

Stand and imagine how grand this church will be when completed. The four 330-foot spires topped with crosses are just a fraction of this mega-church. When finished, the church will have 18 spires. Four will stand at each of the three entrances. Rising above those will be four taller towers, dedicated to the four Evangelists. A tower dedicated to Mary will rise still higher—400 feet. And in the very center of the complex will stand the grand 560-foot Jesus tower, topped with a cross that will shine like a spiritual lighthouse, visible even from out at sea.

The Passion Facade that tourists enter today is only a side entrance to the church. The grand main entrance will be around to the right. That means that the nine-story apartment building will eventually have to be torn down to accommodate it. The three facades—Nativity, Passion,

Nativity Facade—Gaudí completed this side, but much (including the tourist entrance) is unfinished

Sagrada Família

To Hospital
de la Santa Creu i Sant Pau
& Bus #92 to Park Güell

AVINGUDA DE GAUDÍ

Pond

Plaça de Gaudí

20 Meters
20 Yards

Ⓜ Sagrada Família

CARRER DE LA MARINA

Ⓜ Sagrada Família

FENCE

NATIVITY FACADE

❻

⊠ELEV.

❼ MUSEUM

SPIRES

CLOISTER

CARRER DE PROVENÇA

AMBULATORY

CHOIR

T R A N S E P T

NAVE

MODEL

❺

BRONZE DOOR

GLORY FACADE

Ⓑ #19 & #50

❹

SPIRES

CLOISTER

❸

⊠ELEV.

PASSION ❷ FACADE

FENCE

UNFINISHED ESPLANADE

CARRER DE MALLORCA

RAMP

❽ SCHOOL

EXIT

LA CAIXA BANK

Ⓜ Sagrada Família

TICKETS & ENTRANCE

CARRER DE SARDENYA

Ⓣ

Plaça de Sagrada Família

❶

👣 TOUR BEGINS

❶ View of the Exterior
❷ Passion Facade
❸ Atrium
❹ Interior & 4 Red Porphyry Columns

❺ Glory Facade
❻ Nativity Facade
❼ Ramp to Museum
❽ School

and Glory—will chronicle Christ's life from birth to death to resurrection. Despite his boldly modern architectural vision, Gaudí was fundamentally traditional and deeply religious. He designed the Sagrada Família to be a bastion of solid Christian values in a fast-changing city.

Though Gaudí made the original design, he knew it could never be completed in his lifetime. (He enjoyed saying, "My client (God) is not in a hurry.") He gave his blessing to later architects to modify his designs and rely on their own muses for inspiration. But every new plan brings controversy—to stay true to Gaudí's Gothic-Modernista foundation, or use styles that reflect the world today? Discuss.

▶ *Pass through the ticket entrance into the complex, approaching closer to the...*

❷ Passion Facade

Judge for yourself how well Gaudí's original vision has been carried out by later artists. The Passion Facade's four spires were designed by Gaudí and completed (quite faithfully) in 1976. But the lower part was only inspired by Gaudí's designs. The stark sculptures were interpreted freely (and controversially) by Josep Maria Subirachs (b. 1927), who completed the work in 2005.

Subirachs tells the story of Christ's torture and execution. The various scenes—Last Supper, betrayal, whipping, and so on—zigzag up from bottom to top, culminating in Christ's crucifixion over the doorway. The style is severe and unadorned, quite different from Gaudí's signature playfulness. But the bone-like archways are closely based on Gaudí's original designs. And Gaudí had made it clear that this facade should be grim and terrifying.

The facade is full of symbolism. A stylized Alpha-and-Omega is over the door (which faces the setting sun). Jesus, hanging on the cross, has hair made of an open book, symbolizing the word of God. To the left of the door is a grid of numbers, always adding up to 33—Jesus' age at the time of his death. The distinct face of the man below and just left of Christ is a memorial to Gaudí. Now look high above: The two-ton figure suspended between the towers is the soul of Jesus, ascending to heaven.

▶ *Enter the church. As you pass through the ❸ atrium, look down at the fine porphyry floor (with scenes of Jesus' entry into Jerusalem), and look right to see one of the elevators up to the towers. For now, continue into the...*

Passion Facade, with stark, semi-abstract sculpture by Gaudí's successor, Josep Maria Subirachs

The vast nave soars up 150 feet, lined with columns inspired by both Gothic forms and trees

❹ Interior

Typical of even the most traditional Spanish churches, the floor plan is in the shape of a Latin cross, 300 feet long and 200 feet wide. Ultimately, the church will encompass 48,000 square feet, accommodating 8,000 worshippers. The nave's roof is 150 feet high. The crisscross arches of the ceiling (the vaults) show off Gaudí's distinctive engineering. The church's roof and flooring were only completed in 2010—just in time for Pope Benedict XVI to arrive and consecrate the church. As a Catholic church, Sagrada Família is used for services, though irregularly.

Part of Gaudí's religious vision was a love for nature. He said, "Nothing is invented; it's written in nature." Like the trunks of trees, these **columns** (56 in all) blossom with life, complete with branches, leaves, and knot-like capitals. The columns are a variety of colors—brown clay, gray granite, dark-gray basalt. The taller columns are 72 feet tall; the shorter ones are exactly half that.

The angled columns form many **arches.** You'll see both parabolas (U-shaped) and hyperbolas (flatter, elliptical shapes). Gaudí's starting point was the Gothic pointed arch used in medieval churches. But he tweaked it after meticulous study of which arches are best at bearing weight.

Little **windows** let light filter in like the canopy of a rainforest. The clear glass will gradually be replaced by stained glass to match Gaudí's vision of a symphony of colored light.

High up at the back half of the church, the U-shaped **choir**—suspended above the nave—can seat 1,000. The singers will eventually be backed by four organs (there's one now).

Wander through the forest of columns to the center of the church. Here stand four **red porphyry columns,** each marked with an Evangelist's symbol and name in Catalan: angel (Mateu), lion (Marc), bull (Luc), and eagle (Joan). These columns support a ceiling vault that's 200 feet high—and eventually will also support the central steeple, the 560-foot Jesus tower with the shining cross. The steeple will be further supported by four underground pylons, each consisting of 8,000 tons of cement. It will be the tallest church steeple in the world.

Stroll behind the altar through the **ambulatory** to see videos of the 2010 consecration Mass, and look through windows down at the **crypt,** which holds the tomb of Gaudí. There's a move afoot to make Gaudí a saint. Perhaps someday his tomb will be a place of pilgrimage.

Glory Facade's bronze door

Nativity Facade with Jesus in a manger

▶ *Head down the nave to the far end of the church, to what will eventually be the main entrance. Just inside the door, find the* **bronze model** *of the floor plan for the completed church. Facing the doors, look high up to see Subirachs' statue of one of Barcelona's patron saints,* **George** *(Jordi). Go through the doors to imagine what will someday be the...*

❺ Glory Facade

As you exit, study the fine **bronze door,** emblazoned with the Lord's Prayer in Catalan, surrounded by "Give us this day our daily bread" in 50 languages.

Once outside, you'll be face-to-face with...drab, doomed apartment blocks. In the 1950s, the mayor of Barcelona, figuring this day would never really come, sold the land destined for the church project. Now the city must buy back these buildings in order to complete Gaudí's vision. (Today's engineers also struggle with how to shore up the church to withstand the vibrations of speedy AVE trains that rumble underfoot.)

Gaudí envisioned this facade as the main entrance. It will have a grand esplanade leading to this door. Four towers will rise up. The facade's sculpture will represent how the soul passes through death, faces the Last Judgment, avoids the pitfalls of hell, and finds its way to eternal glory with God. Gaudí purposely left the facade's design open for later architects—stay tuned.

▶ *Re-enter the church, backtrack up the nave, and exit out the right transept. Once outside, back up as far as you can to take in the...*

❻ Nativity Facade

This is the only part of the church essentially finished in Gaudí's lifetime. The four spires decorated with his unmistakably non-linear sculpture mark this facade as part of his original design. Mixing Gothic-style symbolism, images from nature, and Modernista asymmetry, the Nativity Facade is the best example of Gaudí's original vision, and it established the template for future architects.

The theme of this facade, which faces the rising sun, is Christ's birth. A statue above the doorway shows Mary, Joseph, and Baby Jesus in the manger, while curious cows peek in. It's the Holy Family—or "Sagrada Família"—for whom this church is dedicated. Flanking the doorway are the three Magi and adoring shepherds. Other statues show Jesus as a young carpenter and angels playing musical instruments. Higher up on the facade, in the arched niche, Jesus crowns Mary triumphantly.

The facade is all about birth and new life, from the dove-covered Tree of Life on top to the turtles at the base of the columns flanking the entrance. There are pelicans (at the base of the tree) and chameleon gargoyles (just above door level). It's as playful as the Passion Facade is grim. Gaudí's plans were for this facade to be painted.

The four **spires** are dedicated to Apostles, and they repeatedly bear the word "Sanctus," or holy. Their colorful ceramic caps symbolize the miters (formal hats) of bishops. They've also come to symbolize Barcelona itself.

▶ *Notice the second **elevator** up to the towers. But for now, head down the ramp to the left of the facade, where you'll find WCs and the entrance to the...*

The Nativity Facade celebrates all life

Gaudí completed this part in his lifetime

❼ Museum

Housed in what will someday be the church's crypt, the museum displays Gaudí's original **models and drawings,** and chronicles the progress of construction over the last 130 years. Wander among the plaster models used for the church's construction, including a model of the nave so big you walk beneath it. You'll notice that the models don't always match the finished product—these are ideas, not blueprints set in stone. The Passion Facade model (near the entrance) shows Gaudí's original vision, with which Subirachs tinkered very freely.

Turn up the main hallway. On the left you can peek into a busy **workshop** still used for making the same kind of plaster models Gaudí used to envision the final product in 3-D. Farther along, a small hallway on the right leads to some original Gaudí architectural **sketches** in a dimly lit room and a worthwhile 20-minute **movie** (generally shown in English at :50 past each hour). From the end of this hall, you have another opportunity to look down into the crypt and at **Gaudí's tomb.**

Back in the main hallway, on the right is the intriguing **"Hanging Model"** for Gaudí's unfinished Church of Colònia Güell (in a suburb of Barcelona), featuring a similar design to the Sagrada Família. The model illustrates how the architect used gravity to calculate the arches that support the church. Wires dangle like suspended chains, forming perfect hyperbolic arches. Attached to these are bags, representing the weight the arches must support. Flip these arches over, and they can bear the heavy weight of the roof. The mirror above the model shows how the right-side-up church is derived from this.

Continue on, beneath a huge plaster model, and turn right to find **three different visions** for this church. Notice how the arches evolved as Gaudí tinkered, from the original, pointy Neo-Gothic arches, to parabolic ones, to the hyperbolic ones he eventually settled on. Before exiting at the far end of the hall, scan the photos (including one of the master himself) and timeline illustrating how construction work has progressed from Gaudí's day to now.

▶ You'll exit near where you started, at the Passion Facade.

❽ School and Rest of Visit

The small building outside the Passion Facade was a school Gaudí erected for the children of the workers building the church. There's a replica of Gaudí's desk as it was the day he died. Pause for a moment to pay homage to the man who made all this possible. Gaudí—a faithful Catholic whose medieval-style mysticism belied his Modernista architecture career—was certainly driven to greatness by his passion for God.

▸ *Our tour is over. To return to central Barcelona, hop on the Metro, or catch a bus along Carrer de Mallorca (by the Glory Facade). Bus #19 stops near the Barcelona Cathedral. Bus #50 goes to the heart of the Eixample (corner of Gran Via de les Corts Catalanes and Passeig de Gràcia), then continues on to Montjuïc.*

Park Güell (✪ see page 130) is two (uphill) miles to the northwest of Sagrada Família. A taxi there costs around €10-12. Or you could take the Metro to Joanic and catch bus #116.

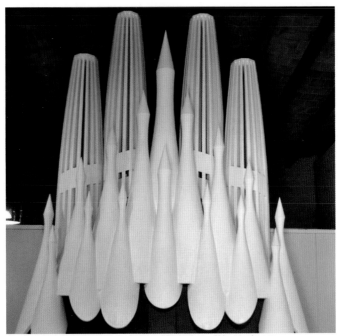

Gaudí's models in the museum give future architects plenty of ideas to chew on

Sights

Barcelona's array of sights is surprisingly varied. There are great walking neighborhoods—the Ramblas, Barri Gòtic, and El Born—for shopping, nightlife, and people-watching. There's the city's Modernista legacy, including Gaudí's Sagrada Família, Casa Milà, and Park Güell. You can also choose from medieval churches and colorful markets, spontaneous outbreaks of folk dancing and quirky museums, Roman ruins and the modern art of Picasso and Miro.

I list sights by neighborhood for handy sightseeing. When you see a ✪ in a listing, it means the sight is covered in much more depth in one of my walks or self-guided tours.

✪ For tips on sightseeing and avoiding lines by making advance reservations, see page 178. Also, be sure to check www.ricksteves.com/update for any significant changes that may have occurred since this book was printed.

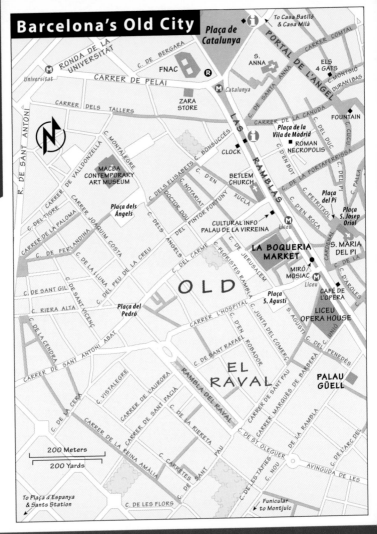

Barcelona's Old City

Plaça de Catalunya

To Casa Batlló & Casa Milà

RONDA DE LA UNIVERSITAT

C. DE BERGARA

PORTAL DE L'ANGEL

CARRER COMTAL

Universitat

C. DE PELAI

FNAC

CARRER DE PELAI

ELS 4 GATS

C. MONTSIÓ

DURAN I BAS

S. ANNA

Catalunya

ZARA STORE

CARRER DELS TALLERS

CARRER DE LA CANUDA

FOUNTAIN

C. DE SANTA ANNA

CARRER DE LA CANUDA

C. DEL DUC

C. CUCU

R. DE SANT ANTONI

CARRER DE VALLDONZELLA

C. MONTALEGRE

C. DE BONSUCCES

Plaça de la Vila de Madrid

ROMAN NECROPOLIS

C. DE LA PORTAFERRISSA

C. DEL PI

C. PALLA

CLOCK

MACBA CONTEMPORARY ART MUSEUM

C. DELS ELISABETS

C. D'EN

BETLEM CHURCH

C. NOTARIAT

C. DEL TIGRE

CARRER JOAQUIM COSTA

DOCTOR DOU

DEL PINTOR FORTUNY

XUCLA

LAS RAMBLAS

C. D'EN BOT

C. D'EN PETRITXOL

Plaça del Pi

Plaça S. Josep Oriol

CARRER DE LA PALOMA

Plaça dels Àngels

C. DELS ÀNGELS

CULTURAL INFO PALAU DE LA VIRREINA

C. D'EN ROCA

S. MARIA DEL PI

CARRER DE FERLANDINA

C. DE LA LLUNA

C. DEL PEU DE LA CREU

C. DEL CARME

C. FLORISTES RAMBLA

C. DE JERUSALEM

LA BOQUERIA MARKET

Liceu

CARDENAL

C. DE LA

C. D'AROLES

C. DE SANT GIL

C. DE SANT VICENÇ

OLD

MIRÓ MOSAIC

Liceu

CAFÉ DE L'OPERA

C. RIERA ALTA

Plaça del Pedró

Plaça S. Agusti

CARRER L'HOSPITAL

C. JUNTA DEL COMERÇ

Plaça S. Agusti

LICEU OPERA HOUSE

C. DE LA CENDRA

C. DE SANT RAFAEL

C. D'EN ROBADOR

C. AGUSTI

C. DEL

C. DE LA UNIÓ

C. DE SANT ANTONI ABAT

EL RAVAL

PENEDÉS

PALAU GÜELL

C. VISTALEGRE

CARRER DE L'AURORA

CARRER DE SANT PAU

CARRER MARQUÈS DE BARBERÀ

DE LA RAMBLA

RAMBLA DEL RAVAL

CARRER DE SANT PACIÀ

C. DE LA RIERETA

C. DE ST. OLEGUER

C. DE LA CERA

200 Meters

200 Yards

CARRER DE LA REINA AMÀLIA

C. CARRETES

DE SANT PAU

C. NOU

AVINGUDA DE LES

To Plaça d'Espanya & Sants Station

C. DE LES FLORS

C. DE LES TÀPIES

Funicular to Montjuïc

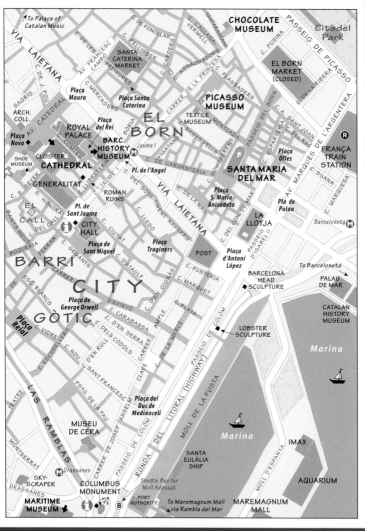

On or Near the Ramblas

▲▲▲The Ramblas

From Plaça de Catalunya to the harborfront, this colorful, pedestrian-friendly boulevard leads through the heart of the Old City. It's a people-watcher's dream.

✪ For a self-guided tour, see the Ramblas Ramble chapter.

▲La Boqueria Market

Discover a wide array of vendors selling Catalan edibles inside this covered hall. It's crowded and touristy but ultra-atmospheric.

✪ See page 25 in the Ramblas Ramble chapter.

▲Palau Güell

This early mansion by Antoni Gaudí shows the architect's first tentative steps toward his trademark curvy style. Even from the outside, you get a sense of this innovative apartment, the first of Gaudí's Modernista buildings. As this is early Gaudí (built 1886-1890), it's darker and more Neo-Gothic than his more famous later projects. The two parabolic-arch doorways and elaborate wrought-iron work signal his emerging nonlinear style.

Inside, you tour intricately decorated living spaces (dining room, bedrooms, and domed central hall) and learn about Gaudí and the Güell family. The highlight is the rooftop, where Gaudí slathered the chimneys with bits of colored glass, tile, and marble to create a forest of giant upside-down ice-cream cones. I'd skip Palau Güell if you plan to see the more interesting Casa Milà (✪ see page 121).

▶ €10, includes engaging audioguide, free first Sun of the month. Open April-Sept Tue-Sun 10:00-20:00, Oct-March Tue-Sun 10:00-17:30, closed Mon year-round, last entry one hour before closing. It's not possible to get advance reservations, so expect some lines. Located a half-block off the Ramblas at Carrer Nou de la Rambla 3-5, Metro: Liceu or Drassanes. Tel. 933-173-974, www.palauguell.cat.

✪ For more on the exterior, see page 30 of the Ramblas Ramble chapter.

▲Plaça Reial

This genteel-feeling square is lined with palm trees and touristy (but still atmospheric) bars and restaurants.

Palau Güell's rooftop chimneys by Gaudí

Maritime Museum, the city's salty legacy

✪ See page 29 in the Ramblas Ramble chapter, and check out recommendations for eateries (✪ page 156) and nightlife (✪ page 182).

▲Maritime Museum (Museu Marítim)

This excellent museum is housed in a well-preserved 14th-century shipyard. The cavernous halls evoke the days when Catalunya's merchant fleet ruled the Mediterranean, and its factories could crank out a galley a week. The permanent collection (which is closed for renovation through 2014) covers the salty history from the 13th to the 20th century—riveting for nautical types and interesting for anyone. Highlights are a huge and richly decorated royal galley, and entrance to the *Santa Eulàlia* schooner docked nearby (on Moll de la Fusta quay).

▶ *Museum—Temporary exhibits only during renovation; price depends on exhibit. Open daily 10:00-20:00, last entry 30 minutes before closing, breezy café in courtyard. Santa Eulàlia—€1 without museum visit, open Tue-Fri and Sun 10:00-19:30, Sat 14:00-19:30, closes at 17:30 Nov-March, closed Mon year-round. Avinguda de la Drassanes, Metro: Drassanes. Tel. 933-429-920, www.mmb.cat.*

Columbus Monument (Monument a Colóm)

This 200-foot-tall monument commemorates Columbus' stop in Barcelona following his first trip to America. An elevator (may be closed) takes you to the top for congested but sweeping views, and there's a small TI inside the monument's base.

✪ See page 30 of the Ramblas Ramble chapter.

Golondrinas **Cruises**

Boats called *golondrinas* take tourists for sightseeing spins around the harbor. As Barcelona's skyline isn't all that striking from the water (and there's no guide), these trips are worthwhile mainly if you just like boat rides.

▶ *Harbor tours—35-minutes-€6.90; 90-minutes-€14.50. Boats run daily 11:30-19:00 May-Oct; less frequent or no departures Nov-April. Located at the harbor, near the Columbus Monument, Metro: Drassanes; ✪ for location see the map on page 4. Tel. 934-423-106, www.lasgolondrinas .com.*

In the Barri Gòtic

Stretching from Plaça de Catalunya to the harbor, the area east of the Ramblas is the old medieval quarter. The closest Metro stop is Jaume I.

For more details on this area and several of the following sights, see the ✪ Barri Gòtic Walk chapter.

▲Cathedral of Barcelona

The city's 14th-century, Gothic-style cathedral (with a Neo-Gothic facade) has played a significant role in Barcelona's history—but as far as grand cathedrals go, this one is relatively unexciting. Still, it's worth a visit to see its richly decorated chapels, finely carved choir, tomb of St. Eulàlia, and restful cloister with gurgling fountains and resident geese.

✪ See the Cathedral of Barcelona Tour chapter.

▲*Sardana* Dances

If you're in town on a weekend, be sure to see the *sardana*, a patriotic dance in which Barcelonans—young and old—link hands and dance in a circle. For some it's a highly symbolic, politically charged action representing Catalan unity—but for most it's just a fun chance to kick up their heels. Participants put their belongings in the center, join hands, and hop and sway to the music, *Zorba the Greek*-style, while the band plays odd-looking oboes, brass instruments, and bongos. All are welcome, even tourists with two left feet.

▶ *The free dances, which last an hour or two, are held in the square in front of the cathedral on Sundays at 12:00 and usually also Saturdays at 18:00 (none in Aug; Metro: Jaume I).*

Locals and tourists dance the *sardana*

Frederic Marès Museum—more than statues

Frederic Marès Museum (Museu Frederic Marès)

This eclectic collection assembled by local sculptor and packrat Frederic Marès (1893-1991) sprawls around a peaceful courtyard. There's lots of sculpture, from ancient to Gothic to the early 20th century. More interesting is Marès' "Collector's Cabinet" of everyday 19th-century bric-a-brac: rooms upon rooms of scissors, fans, nutcrackers, stamps, pipes, snuff boxes, pocket watches, bicycles, and dolls. And in Marès' study are several sculptures by the artist himself. The tranquil courtyard café (summer only, until 22:00) offers a pleasant break, even when the museum is closed.

▸ *€4.20, free Sun from 15:00, audioguide-€1. Open Tue-Sat 10:00-19:00, Sun 11:00-20:00, closed Mon. Located to the left of the cathedral at Plaça de Sant Iu 5-6, Metro: Jaume I. Tel. 932-563-500, www.museu mares.bcn.cat.*

Shoe Museum (Museu del Calçat)

Shoe lovers enjoy this tiny museum of footwear in glass display cases, watched over by an earnest attendant. You'll see shoes from the 1700s to today: fancy ladies' boots, Tibetan moccasins, big clown shoes, and shoes of minor celebrities such as the president of Catalunya. The huge shoes at the entry are designed to fit the feet of the statue atop the Columbus Monument at the bottom of the Ramblas.

▸ *€2.50. Open Tue-Sun 11:00-14:00, closed Mon. Plaça Sant Felip Neri 5, Metro: Jaume I. Tel. 933-014-533.*

Roman Temple of Augustus (Temple Roma d'August)

Tucked inside a small medieval courtyard, four columns from an ancient temple of Augustus are a reminder of Barcelona's Roman origins.

⭐ See page 48 of the Barri Gòtic Walk chapter.

▲Barcelona History Museum
(Museu d'Història de Barcelona: Plaça del Rei)

Barcelona has thrived for 2,500 years. It's been a Roman retirement colony, a maritime power, a dynamo of the Industrial Age, and a cradle for all things modern. This museum—housed in medieval buildings that rise over excavated Roman ruins—lets you walk through that history. Posted information is only in Catalan and Spanish, but the included English audioguide provides informative, if dry, descriptions.

Start with the 10-minute introductory video on the first floor; it plays alternately in Catalan, Spanish, and English. Then take an elevator down 65 feet (and 2,000 years) to stroll the ruins of Roman Barcino. You'll see models of domestic life, plus the remains of sewers, a fish-processing factory, winemaking facilities, and bits of an early Christian church.

On the ground floor, in an 11th-century count's palace, you see exhibits on Barcelona's medieval days as a sea-trading empire.

Finally, head upstairs to see a model of the city from the early 16th century. From here, you can also enter Tinell Hall (part of the former Royal Palace), with its long, graceful, rounded vaults. Nearby, step into the 14th-century Chapel of St. Agatha, to soak up the medieval ambience of Barcelona's glory days.

▸ *€7, includes audioguide, free all day first Sun of month and other Sun from 15:00—but no audioguide during free times. Open Tue-Sat 10:00-19:00, Sun 10:00-20:00, closed Mon; last entry 30 minutes before closing. Located on Plaça del Rei, enter on Vageur street, Metro: Jaume I. Tel. 932-562-122, www.museuhistoria.bcn.cat.*

▲▲Palace of Catalan Music (Palau de la Música Catalana)

This concert hall, built in just three years and finished in 1908, features an unexceptional exterior but boasts my favorite Modernista interior in town (by Lluís Domènech i Montaner). Its inviting arches lead you into the 2,138-seat hall. A kaleidoscopic skylight features a choir singing around the sun, while playful carvings and mosaics celebrate music and Catalan culture. If you're interested in Modernisme, it's one of the best experiences in town—and helps balance the hard-to-avoid fixation on Gaudí as "Mr. Modernisme."

Unless you attend a performance at the hall, you must take a tour to get inside (reserve in advance).

▶ *€15. 50-minute tours in English run daily every hour 10:00-15:00, tour times may change based on performance schedule, reserve tour tickets in person at the hall (open daily 9:30-15:30), by phone with a credit card (tel. 902-475-485), or online at www.palaumusica.cat (€1 fee). Located about six blocks northeast of the cathedral at Carrer Palau de la Música 4-6, Metro: Urquinaona.*

Concerts: *Music lovers see the hall's interior while attending a concert (300 per year, €22-49 tickets, see www.palaumusica.cat for schedule, box office tel. 902-442-882).*

El Born and Nearby

The neighborhood called El Born (also known as La Ribera) is a bohemian-chic paradise of funky shops, upscale eateries, a colorful market hall, unique boutiques, the Picasso Museum, and rollicking nightlife. It feels wonderfully local, with a higher ratio of Barcelonans to tourists than most other city-center zones. The heart of the neighborhood is the narrow lanes sprouting around Passeig del Born and the Church of Santa Maria del Mar (Metro: Jaume I).

▲El Born Walk

Stroll through this rough-but-gentrifying neighborhood from the Cathedral of Barcelona to the Church of Santa Maria del Mar. I'll only give directions, not lengthy descriptions, and let El Born's authenticity speak for itself.

Facing the **cathedral,** turn left. As you cross Plaça d'Antoni Maura

Palace of Catalan Music, a Modernista gem

Santa Caterina Market in El Born

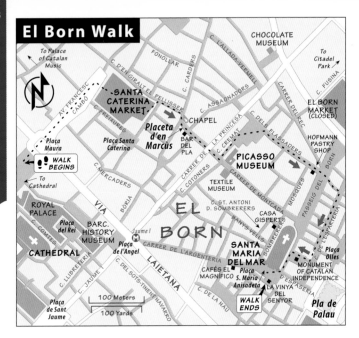

and traffic-choked Via Laietana, you enter El Born. Continue toward the undulating roof of **Santa Caterina Market.** It's the local choice for buying *jamón*, cheese, and colorful produce, and a good place to enjoy inviting eateries (for more on the market, see the listing later in this section).

Pass through the market and exit out its back end, angle left, then turn right on tiny Carrer d'en Giralt el Pellisser. Continue past the humble 12th-century church (supposedly Barcelona's oldest) until the street becomes **Carrer de Montacada**—lined with art galleries, shops, and eateries.

Just after crossing Carrer de la Princesa (before you reach the Picasso Museum), turn left down the covered passage marked *Carrer de Cremat Gran i Xic.* Emerging at a leafy square, turn right down **Carrer dels Flassaders.** Here and on side streets, many shops actually produce their goods on the premises. Hofmann (at Flassaders #44) is the pastry shop for Barcelona's best-regarded culinary school.

Cross **Passeig del Born,** the long boulevard that's the neighborhood hub for nightlife in the surrounding lanes. Continue straight, down an arcaded street, then turn right along **Carrer de l'Esparteria.** Explore this area and its side streets, rich with fashion boutiques, local craftsmen, and laundry drying from wrought-iron balconies—classic Barcelona.

Turn right down Carrer del Malcuinat, to the **Monument of Catalan Independence.** This marks the site of a mass grave. On September 11, 1714, Bourbon King Philip V conquered independent Barcelona, massacred the resisters, and established two centuries of dominance by the Madrid government. Catalan language and culture were outlawed. Today Catalunya is thriving, but the monument's flame burns eternally for the "Catalan Alamo," and 9/11 remains a sobering anniversary. (When Catalans head to the toilet, they still say, "I'm going to Philip's house.")

The 14th-century **Church of Santa Maria del Mar** anchors El Born. The unadorned interior—naked in all its pure Catalan-Gothic glory—features tree-like columns that inspired Gaudí's Sagrada Família, colorful chapels, and modern stained-glass windows. For more on the church, see the listing later in this section.

Near the church, you can sip a drink at La Vinya del Senyor wine bar (facing the church entrance), buy a bottle at Vila Vinateca wine shop (Carrer des Agullers 7), sample the city's "best" coffee at Cafés El Magnífico (Carrer de l'Argenteria 64), and inhale roasting nuts at Casa Gispert (Carrer dels Sombrerers 23). You're at the heart of Barcelona's most colorful bohemian quarter.

▲▲▲Picasso Museum (Museu Picasso)

Pablo Picasso may have made his career in Paris, but the years he spent in Barcelona—from ages 14 through 23—were among the most formative of his life. The museum focuses on those early years, while including a few representative works spanning his long life. It's undoubtedly the top collection of Picassos in his native country.

✪ See the Picasso Museum Tour chapter.

▲Santa Caterina Market

This eye-catching market hall's colorful, rippling roof (2006) covers a delightful shopping zone that caters more to locals than to tourists. Come for the outlandish architecture, but stay for a chance to shop for a picnic without the tourist logjam of La Boqueria Market on the Ramblas. Besides fresh produce, it has many inviting eateries.

▶ *Free. Open Mon 7:30-14:00, Tue-Wed and Sat 7:30-15:30, Thu-Fri 7:30-20:30, closed Sun. Avinguda de Francesc Cambó 16, Metro: Jaume I. Tel. 933-195-740, www.mercatsantacaterina.net.*

▲Church of Santa Maria del Mar

This 14th-century church is the proud centerpiece of El Born. The "Cathedral of the Sea" was built entirely with local funds by wealthy shippers and merchants.

On the big front doors, notice the figures of workers who donated their time and sweat to build the church. The stone for the church was quarried at Montjuïc and had to be carried across town on the backs of porters.

Step inside. The church features a purely Catalan Gothic interior. During the Spanish Civil War (1936-1939), Catalan patriots fighting Franco burned the ornate Baroque decoration (carbon still blackens the ceiling), leaving behind this unadorned Gothic. The colorful windows come with modern themes. The tree-like columns inspired Gaudí's work on Sagrada Família. Befitting a church "of the sea," sailors traditionally left models of ships at the altar to win Mary's protection—one remains today.

▶ *Free. Open daily 9:00-13:30 & 16:30-20:00. Plaça Santa Maria 1, Metro: Jaume I. Tel. 933-102-390.*

Chocolate Museum (Museu de la Xocolata)

Fun for chocolate lovers, this museum tells the story of chocolate from Aztecs to Europeans via the port of Barcelona, where it was first unloaded and processed. But the history lesson is just an excuse to show off some remarkably ornate candy sculptures. These works of edible art—which change every year but often include such themes as Don Quixote or the roofs of Barcelona—are displayed in store windows for Easter or Christmas.

▶ *€4.30. Open Mon-Sat 10:00-19:00, Sun 10:00-15:00. Located a few blocks from the Picasso Museum at Carrer del Comerç 36, Metro: Jaume I. Tel. 932-687-878, www.museuxocolata.cat.*

Citadel Park (Parc de la Ciutadella)

In 1888, the site of a much-hated military citadel (representing the Madrid government's oppression) was transformed into the fairgrounds of an international exposition. The stately Triumphal Arch at the top of the park, celebrating the removal of the citadel, was the main entrance.

Today the Citadel is Barcelona's biggest, greenest park, complete with a zoo and museums of geology and zoology. It's a haven (especially on weekends) for happy families escaping the concrete and population density of modern Barcelona. Enjoy the ornamental fountain that the young Antoni Gaudí helped design, and consider renting a rowboat on the lake in the center of the park. Check out the tropical Umbracle greenhouse and the Hivernacle winter garden, which has a pleasant café. The zoo features tigers, hippos, and zebras plus a SeaWorld-like dolphin show.

▶ *Park—open daily 10:00 until dusk. Zoo—adults-€17, kids 3-12-€10.20, open daily in summer 10:00-20:00, shorter hours off-season, tel. 902-457-545, www.zoobarcelona.cat. Metro: Arc de Triomf, Barceloneta, or Ciutadella-Vila Olímpica.*

▲Barcelona's Beaches

This man-made Riviera is great for sunbathing or an evening paseo before dinner. Barcelona's beaches are like a resort island—complete with lounge chairs, volleyball, showers, WCs, and inviting beach bars called *chiringuitos*. Bike paths make the beaches great for joy-riding (✪ see page 176 for bike-rental places).

▶ *Located east of the El Born neighborhood, the sand starts in Barceloneta and stretches north. Metro: Barceloneta; also bus #36.*

Santa Maria del Mar—"Catalan Gothic"

Take a vacation from museums at the beach

The Eixample

The grid-patterned neighborhood north of Plaça de Catalunya (Metro: Passeig de Gràcia) is dotted with buildings in the Modernista style and brims with upscale stores and eateries. ✪ For more about this neighborhood, see the Eixample Walk chapter.

▲Block of Discord

Three colorful Modernista facades—at Casa Batlló, Casa Amatller, and Casa Lleó Morera—by three different architects create a delightful "discord" along a single city block. If you're tempted to snap photos from the middle of the street, be careful: Gaudí died after being struck by a streetcar.

▶ *Free to view from the outside. Located on Passeig de Gràcia (at the Metro stop of the same name), between Carrer del Consell de Cent and Carrer d'Aragó.*

✪ For more about the Block of Discord, see page 88 of the Eixample Walk chapter.

▲Casa Batlló

Gaudí's creation is the only Block of Discord building you can enter. The over-the-top interior is even more interesting than Casa Milà's. The house features a funky mushroom-shaped fireplace nook on the main floor, a blue-and-white-ceramic-slathered atrium, and an attic with parabolic arches—there's barely a straight line in the house. You can also get a close-up look at the dragon-inspired rooftop. Because preservation of the place is privately funded, the entrance fee is steep.

▶ *€18.15, includes good audioguide. Open daily 9:00-20:00, may close*

Block of Discord—three frisky facades

Casa Milà's parabola-shaped attic

Modernista Sights

For some visitors, Modernista architecture is Barcelona's main draw. Showpieces of the movement—the Block of Discord and Gaudí's Casa Milà—can be seen in the Eixample neighborhood. Nearby are two lesser-known works by Lluís Domènech i Montaner: Fundació Antoni Tàpies (around the corner from the Block of Discord, at Carrer d'Aragó 255) and Hotel Casa Fuster (directly across Avinguda de Diagonal, at the far end of a small park at Passeig de Gràcia 132). Also in the Eixample are two buildings by Josep Puig i Cadafalch: Palau Baró de Quadras (a few blocks east from the top of Passeig de Gràcia at Diagonal #373) and Casa de les Punxes ("House of Spikes," at #416).

At the northern edge of the Eixample is Gaudí's greatest piece of work, the yet-to-be-finished Sagrada Família church. Farther north is Park Güell, where Gaudí put his colorful stamp on 30 acres of greenery.

Other Modernista highlights include Gaudí's Palau Güell, just off the Ramblas (see page 110); Lluís Domènech i Montaner's Palace of Catalan Music in El Born (✪ see page 114); and Josep Puig i Cadafalch's CaixaForum, at the base of Montjuïc (✪ see page 128). For information on Modernista sights, visit the TI on Plaça de Catalunya, which has a special desk just for Modernisme maniacs.

early for special events. Purchase a ticket online in advance to skip to the head of the line (especially long in the morning). Passeig de Gràcia 41, Metro: Passeig de Gràcia. Tel. 932-160-306, www.casabatllo.cat.

✪ For more on the exterior, see page 88 of the Eixample Walk chapter.

▲▲Casa Milà (La Pedrera)

This corner house, located three blocks from the Block of Discord (toward Avinguda de Diagonal), is one of Gaudí's trademark works and an icon of Modernisme. It's worth going inside, as it's arguably the purest Gaudí interior in town. It was executed at the height of his abilities (unlike his earlier Palau Güell) and still contains original furnishings.

The typical bourgeois **apartment** you'll visit is decorated as it might have been by its first middle-class owners. A seven-minute video explains

Barcelona society at the time. Notice Gaudí's clever use of the curvaceous atrium to maximize daylight.

In the **attic,** under parabola-shaped arches that support the roof, a sprawling multimedia exhibit traces the architect's career. Finally you reach the undulating, jaw-dropping **rooftop** and fine views. (Make sure you budget enough time to enjoy the roof, and note that it may close when it rains.) Explore this forest of playful, sculpted towers, where 30 chimneys play volleyball with the clouds.

▶ *€15, good audioguide-€4. Open daily March-Oct 9:00-20:00, Nov-Feb 9:00-18:30, last entry 30 minutes before closing. Located at the corner of Passeig de Gràcia and Provença, at Provença 261-265, Metro: Diagonal. Info tel. 902-400-973.*

Avoiding Lines: Avoid a wait (up to 1.5 hours) by reserving an assigned entry time at www.lapedrera.com or at a CaixaCatalunya ATM, or by buying a skip-the-line Articket BCN pass (✪ see page 178). Otherwise, it's least crowded right at opening time.

Free Entrance to Atrium: The door directly on the corner leads to the main atrium and, upstairs on the first floor, temporary exhibits.

Nighttime Visits: Pricey after-hours visits (generally 21:30-24:00), dubbed "The Secret Pedrera," let you tour with the lights down low. On summer weekends, Casa Milà hosts a rooftop concert series, "Summer Nights at La Pedrera."

✪ For more on the exterior, see page 91 of the Eixample Walk chapter.

Montjuïc

Montjuïc (mohn-jew-EEK, "Mount of the Jews"), the hill overlooking Barcelona's hazy port, offers a park-like setting that's home to a variety of good (if not knockout) sights. You could lace together a number of them in a day of sightseeing, or just focus on one or two.

Getting to Montjuïc: A taxi directly to your destination costs about €7 from downtown. Buses #50 and #193 leave from Plaça d'Espanya and hit most of the sights. The red Tourist Bus from Plaça de Catalunya also swings by the main sights. A funicular goes up from the Paral-lel Metro stop (covered by Metro ticket). From the top of the funicular, you can walk to several sights, or catch a cable car up to the castle (€7 one-way, €10 round-trip). (Another cable car line, from the tip of the Barceloneta peninsula, is scenic but ex-cru-ci-a-ting-ly slow.) If you only want to go to the

Fundació Joan Miró, on Montjuïc

550-foot Montjuïc overlooks the harbor

base of the hill (Catalan Art Museum and CaixaForum), you can ride the escalators from Plaça d'Espanya.

Getting Around Montjuïc: The various sights are (more or less) a quarter-mile apart. It's easy to walk between them along streets and paths—especially downhill. You can also connect the sights using the red Tourist Bus, public bus #193, or bus #55 (though it skips the castle). To see all the sights, ride up to the castle (by taxi, bus, or funicular/cable car), then walk or ride downhill, seeing them in the order below.

Castle of Montjuïc

While just an empty brick-and-concrete shell today, the castle offers great city views from its ramparts. It was built in the 18th century by the central Spanish government to keep an eye on rebellious Barcelona. Survey the Mediterranean and the boats in the harbor: container ships, ferries to Mallorca, and cruise ships. To the left is the former industrial zone that's now a swanky stretch of beaches and fancy condos. To the right is Spain's leading port, with containers that stretch all the way to the airport.

▶ *Free. Open daily 9:00-21:00 (until 19:00 Oct-March). To get there, take a taxi, bus #193 from Plaça d'Espanya, or the funicular-plus-cable car from Metro: Paral·lel.*

▲Fundació Joan Miró

This is the best collection anywhere of work by the pioneering abstract artist Joan Miró (1893-1983). It's an always-changing, loosely chronological overview of Miró's oeuvre, plus excellent temporary exhibits.

Born in Barcelona, Miró divided his time between Paris and Catalunya. His style is simple and childlike, with shapes that suggest the

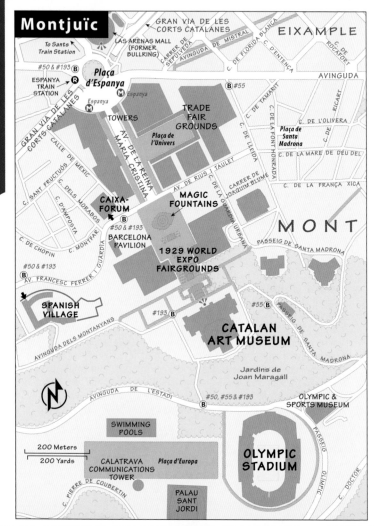

Montjuïc

GRAN VIA DE LES CORTS CATALANES

EIXAMPLE

To Sants Train Station

#50 & #193

LAS ARENAS MALL (FORMER BULLRING)

CARRER DE SEPÚLVEDA

AVINGUDA DE MISTRAL

C. DE FLORIDA BLANCA

C. D'ENTENÇA

C. DE ROCAFORT

ESPANYA TRAIN STATION

R

Plaça d'Espanya

M Espanya

AVINGUDA

GRAN VIA DE LES CORTS CATALANES

M Espanya

TOWERS

B #55

C. DE TAMARIT

C. DE L'OLIVERA

C. DE LA FONT HONRADA

C. DE RICART

Plaça de Santa Madrona

C. DE

AV. DE LA REINA MARIA CRISTINA

TRADE FAIR GROUNDS

Plaça de l'Univers

C. DE LLEIDA

C. DE LA MARE DE DÉU DEL

CALLE DE MÉXICO

C. SANT FRUCTUÓS

C. DELS MORABOS

C. D'AMPOSTA

AV. DE RIUS I TAULET

CARRER DE JOAQUIM BLUME

C. DE LA FRANÇA XICA

CAIXA-FORUM

B

MAGIC FOUNTAINS

C. DE LA GUARDIA URBANA

MONT

#50 & #193

Barcelona Pavilion

PASSEIG DE SANTA MADRONA

C. DE CHOPIN

C. MONTFAR

1929 WORLD EXPO FAIRGROUNDS

#50 & #193

B

AV. FRANCESC FERRER I GUÀRDIA

SPANISH VILLAGE

#193 B

#55 B

PASSEIG DE SANTA MADRONA

CATALAN ART MUSEUM

AVINGUDA DELS MONTANYANS

Jardins de Joan Maragall

N

AVINGUDA DE L'ESTADI

#50, #55 & #193

OLYMPIC & SPORTS MUSEUM

PASSEIG OLÍMPIC

SWIMMING POOLS

200 Meters

200 Yards

CALATRAVA COMMUNICATIONS TOWER

Plaça d'Europa

OLYMPIC STADIUM

C. PIERRE DE COUBERTIN

PALAU SANT JORDI

C. DOCTOR

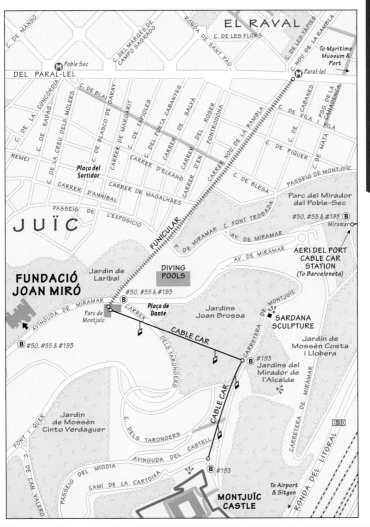

EL RAVAL

C. DE LES FLORS

To Maritime
Museum &
Port

Poble Sec

DEL PARAL-LEL

Paral-lel

C. DE MANSO

C. DEL MARQÈS DE CAMPO SAGRADO

RONDA DE SANT PAU

C. NOU DE LA RAMBLA

C. DE LES TÀPIES

C. DE BLAI

C. DE BLASCO DE GARAY

C. DE LA CONCORDIA

C. DE LA RABAS

C. DE LA CREU DELS MOLERS

REMEI

Plaça del Sortidor

C. D'ANNIBAL

PASSEIG DE L'EXPOSICIÓ

JUÏC

CARRER DE MARGARIT

C. DEL POETA CABANYES

CARRER DE TÀPIOLES

CARRER DE SALVÀ

CARRER DEL ROSER

FONTRODONA

CARRER D'ELKANO

CARRER D'EN

CARRER NOU DE LA RAMBLA

C. DE BLESA

CARRER DE MAGALHAES

C. DE CABANES

C. DE VILA I VILA

PSG. DE LA CANADENCA

C. DE PIQUER

C. DE MATA

PASSEIG DE MONTJUIC

Parc del Mirador
del Poble-Sec

#50, #55 & #193

C. FONT TROBADA

AV. DE MIRAMAR

PG. DE MIRAMAR

Miramar

AERI DEL PORT
CABLE CAR
STATION
(To Barceloneta)

FUNICULAR

DIVING POOLS

Jardin de
Laribal

AV. DE MIRAMAR

FUNDACIÓ
JOAN MIRÓ

AVINGUDA DE MIRAMAR

#50, #55 & #193

Parc de Montjuïc

Plaça de Dante

CARRER

CABLE CAR

Jardins
Joan Brossa

CARRETERA DE MONTJUÏC

SARDANA
SCULPTURE

Jardin de
Mossèn Costa
i Llobera

#50, #55 & #193

DELS TARONGERS

#193

Jardíns del
Mirador de
l'Alcalde

CABLE CAR

CARRETERA DE MIRAMAR

Jardin de Mossèn
Cinto Verdaguer

C. DELS TARONGERS

FONT I QUER

C. DE CAN VALERO

PASSEIG DEL MIGDIA

AVINGUDA DEL CASTELL

CAMÍ DE LA CARTOIXA

B-10

RONDA DEL LITORAL

#193

MONTJUÏC
CASTLE

To Airport
& Sitges

basic elements of the cosmos—things like stars, people, music, love. To appreciate Miró's art, try this: Meditate on it, then read the title (for example, *The Smile of a Tear*), then meditate again. Rinse and repeat until you have an epiphany. There's no correct answer—it's pure poetry.

The permanent collection starts on the main floor. Room 11 has the 400-square-foot *Tapestry of the Foundation* (1979) that Miró designed for this space. Notice his trademark star and moon. Nearby, detour downstairs for a 15-minute film about Miró.

Room 16 traces young Miró's artistic development, as he experiments with Fauvism, Cubism, Catalan folk art, and Impressionism. In 1920, he traveled to Paris, dabbled in Dada, and socialized with Surrealists. Like them, Miró's work tries to circumvent the viewer's preconceptions by juxtaposing unlikely images in order to short-circuit the brain. His Green Paintings (1925-1927) became increasingly abstract, replacing photo-realistic images with abstract symbols on a flat background. By 1925, Miró was leaving the figurative world behind, painting a completely abstract, uninterpretable canvas, cheekily titled "*Painting.*"

Head upstairs to the second floor. With the advent of the Spanish Civil War, Miró temporarily revived his figurative style to depict the monsters of war (Wind Paintings, 1930s). In the 1940s, he became fixated on the heavens, producing his Constellations series, featuring colorful stars and moons on bright backgrounds. The Sixties Gallery shows him refining his signature style, stripping everything down to the basics. Star. Moon. Bird. Woman.

Some of Miró's best work can't be found in any museum—it's scattered around the streets of Barcelona, including the center of the Ramblas (✪ see page 27).

▶ *€10, great €4 audioguide. Open Tue-Sat 10:00-20:00 (until 19:00 Oct-June), Thu until 21:30, Sun 10:00-14:30, closed Mon year-round. Located 200 yards from top of funicular. Tel. 934-439-470, www.fundacio miro-bcn.org.*

Olympic Stadium (Estadi Olímpic) and Sports Museum (Museu Olímpic i de l'Esport)

Barcelona's Olympic Stadium offers little to see today, but if the doors are open, you're welcome to step inside. Originally built for the 1929 World Expo, the stadium was updated for the 1992 Summer Olympics. At the opening ceremonies, an archer dramatically lit the Olympic torch—which still stands high—with a flaming arrow. This was the Olympics of the US basketball "Dream Team" (Michael Jordan and company), and the first after the fall of the Soviet Union. The futuristic communications tower is by the famous Spanish architect Santiago Calatrava.

Next door, at the Sports Museum, you'll twist down a timeline-ramp that traces the history of the Olympic Games. Downstairs, you'll find exhibits that test your athleticism, remember the '92 Games, and honor Juan Antonio Samaranch, the influential Catalan president of the IOC for two decades. High-tech but hokey, the museum is worth it only for those nostalgic for the '92 Games.

▶ *€4.50. Open April-Sept Tue-Sat 10:00-20:00 (until 18:00 Oct-March), Sun 10:00-14:30, closed Mon year-round. Located at Avinguda de l'Estadi 60. Tel. 932-925-379, www.fundaciobarcelonaolimpica.es.*

▲▲Catalan Art Museum (Museu Nacional d'Art de Catalunya)

The "MNAC" is often called "the Prado of Romanesque art" for its world-class medieval frescoes. It's also a sweep through Catalan art from the 10th to the 20th century. For art aficionados—but not necessarily everyone else—this is a major sight.

The Romanesque art (in the left wing of the museum) came mostly from remote Catalan village churches high in the Pyrenees. You'll see frescoes, statues, and painted wooden altar fronts—with flat 2-D scenes, each saint holding his symbol, and Jesus with his cross-shaped halo—all displayed in replica church settings.

The Gothic murals (right wing) evolve into vivid 14th-century wood-panel paintings of Bible stories. Don't miss the Catalan master

Olympic Stadium of 1929 and 1992 Games

Catalan Art Museum has medieval frescoes

Jaume Huguet (1412-1492) and his *Consecration of St. Agustí Vell* (in Room 26).

Upstairs, the Renaissance and Baroque section covers Spain's Golden Age—Zurbarán, heavy religious scenes, and Spanish royals with their endearing underbites. In the Modern section, circle clockwise for a short chronological tour through Symbolism, Modernisme, Art Deco, and more. Catalan artist Ramon Casas (and his Toulouse-Lautrec-esque works) had a profound impact on young Picasso. In the "Modern 2" section, you'll find Modernist-era furniture, Impressionism, and several distinctly Picasso portraits of women.

The museum also has a coin collection and the chic Oleum restaurant, with vast city views.

▸ *€10, free first Sun of month. Open Tue-Sat 10:00-19:00, Sun 10:00-14:30, closed Mon, last entry 30 minutes before closing. Located above the Magic Fountains near Plaça d'Espanya—take the escalators up. Tel. 936-220-376, www.mnac.cat.*

▲World Expo Fairgrounds, Plaça d'Espanya, and More

Stretching from Plaça d'Espanya to the base of Montjuïc, this sprawling cluster of buildings, fountains, plazas, and esplanades was originally built for the 1929 World Expo. Today it's part of an impressive neighborhood of old and new buildings that create some wonderful public spaces. It's worth a visit for its architecture (Modernista, Art Deco, and Modern), and for glimpses into Barcelona today. It's free to stroll the grounds, starting either from Plaça d'Espanya (convenient Metro stop) or as you descend from Montjuïc.

▲Magic Fountains (Font Màgica): Music, colored lights, and huge amounts of water make an artistic splash many evenings.

▸ *Free 20-minute shows start on the half-hour. They almost always play May-Sept Thu-Sun 21:00-23:00, no shows Mon-Wed; Oct-April Fri-Sat 19:00-20:30, no shows Sun-Thu. From the Espanya Metro stop, walk toward the towering National Palace on the hill.*

▲▲CaixaForum: One of Barcelona's most important Art Nouveau buildings—by Josep Puig i Cadafalch (✪ see page 87)—was built as a state-of-the-art textile factory. In 2002, it reopened as a cultural center, bringing art to the people for free. Ride the escalator to the first floor for a permanent display about the building, then explore the temporary exhibits.

The Modernista Terrace boasts a wavy floor, bristling with fanciful brick towers, and offers great views. Across the street is Ludwig Mies van der Rohe's Barcelona Pavilion, an austere building that demonstrates the contrast between minimalist "Modern" architecture and the more ornamented "Modernista" style.

▸ *Free. Open Mon-Fri 10:00-20:00, Sat-Sun 10:00-21:00, July-Aug open late on some days—likely Wed until 23:00. Avinguda de Francesc Ferrer i Guàrdia 6-8. Tel. 934-768-600, http://obrasocial.lacaixa.es—click on "CaixaForum Barcelona."*

Spanish Village (Poble Espanyol): A tacky and overpriced five-acre faux village (complete with craftspeople selling trinkets), built for the 1929 World Expo to show off the "real" Spain.

▸ *€11. Open daily 9:00-20:00 or later, closes earlier off-season. Avinguda de Francesc Ferrer i Guàrdia 6-8, Metro: Espanya. Tel. 935-086-300, www.poble-espanyol.com.*

▲**Las Arenas (Bullring Mall):** What do you do with a big arena when your society decides to outlaw bullfighting? Make a mall. The former bullfight ring has become a home to chain stores, a multiplex, a food-circus basement, a rock-and-roll museum, and a roof terrace with stupendous views of Plaça d'Espanya and Montjuïc (reachable by external glass elevator for €1 or from inside for free).

▸ *Free. Open daily 10:00-22:00. Gran Via de les Corts Catalanes 373-385, Metro: Espanya. Tel. 982-890-244, www.arenasdebarcelona.com.*

World Expo Fairgrounds, Plaça d'Espanya

Las Arenas—bullring turned shopping mall

Away from the Center

▲▲▲Sagrada Família (Holy Family Church)

Antoni Gaudí's grand masterpiece sits unfinished in a residential Eixample neighborhood 1.5 miles north of Plaça de Catalunya. Its soaring spires and melting-in-the-rain facades are an icon of the city.

   ✪ See the Sagrada Família Tour chapter.

▲▲Park Güell

Tucked in the foothills at the northwest edge of Barcelona, this fanciful park—designed by Antoni Gaudí—combines playful design, inviting public spaces, a pleasant park-like setting (amid a busy city), and sweeping views. Begun in 1900, it was intended to be a 30-acre, 60-residence gated community for Barcelona's *nouveaux riches*, including the developer Eusebi Güell (pronounced "gway"). With World War I, progress stalled, and the place became a park for fans of Gaudí and Modernisme.

At the **main entrance,** walk through a palm-frond gate, past two Hansel-and-Gretel gingerbread houses that announce this is a magical space. (One house is a good bookshop; the other a skippable museum.)

Now climb the **main staircase.** The caves on either side were garages for Güell's newfangled automobiles. You'll pass the famous dragon fountain of St. George that's become an icon of the city.

At the top is the **Hall of 100 Columns** (actually 86), the produce market for the housing development. On the ceiling are four giant sun-like decorations (the four seasons), designed to hold lanterns from their hooks. Here and elsewhere are surfaces covered with Modernisme's signature

Park Güell stairs to Hall of 100 Columns

Park Güell terrace has a great city view

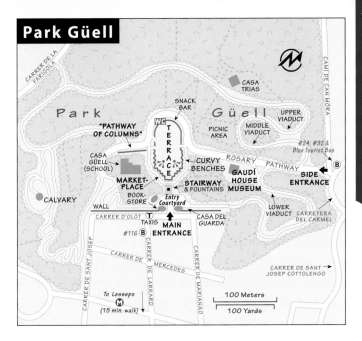

Park Güell

Park Güell

CARRER DE LA FARIGOLA

CASA TRIAS

SNACK BAR

"PATHWAY OF COLUMNS"

UPPER VIADUCT

MIDDLE VIADUCT

PICNIC AREA

WC

TERRACE

CASA GÜELL (SCHOOL)

CURVY BENCHES

ROSARY PATHWAY

#24, #92 & Blue Tourist Bus

MARKET-PLACE

GAUDÍ HOUSE MUSEUM

SIDE ENTRANCE

STAIRWAY & FOUNTAINS

CALVARY

BOOK-STORE

Entry Courtyard

WALL

CARRER D'OLOT

LOWER VIADUCT

CARRETERA DEL CARMEL

TAXIS

CASA DEL GUARDA

#116 B

MAIN ENTRANCE

CAMÍ DE CAN MORA

B

Sights

CARRER DE SANT JOSEP

CARRER DE LARRARD

CARRER DE MERCEDES

CARRER DE MARIANAO

CARRER DE SANT JOSEP COTTOLENGO

To Lesseps (15 min. walk)

100 Meters

100 Yards

trencadís mosaics—colorful bits of broken dishes and discarded tile. Though Gaudí became famous for the technique, most of this was executed by his collaborator, Josep Maria Jujol.

Continue up the left-hand staircase, looking left, down the playful **Pathway of Columns.** Gaudí drew his inspiration from nature, and this arcade is like a surfer's perfect tube. Gaudí intended for cars to travel across the top, with pedestrians in the arcade below.

Continuing up, you pop out on the **terrace.** Sit on the colorful, undulating, 360-foot-long bench and enjoy one of Barcelona's best views. (Find Gaudí's Sagrada Família church in the distance.) The terrace was to be the community's wide-open meeting place. Gaudí engineered a system to catch the terrace's rainwater runoff and funnel it down into a 300,000-gallon cistern. The water was bottled and sold; excess water powers the park's fountains.

The pink house with a steeple was Gaudí's home for the 20 years he worked here, though Gaudí did not design it. Today it's the **Gaudí House Museum** with some quirky Gaudí furniture.

The park's highest point is the **Calvary,** a stubby stone tower with three crosses representing the hill where Christ was crucified. Gaudí envisioned the topography of Park Güell as a spiritual journey—starting at the low end and toiling upward to reach spiritual enlightenment. If not enlightenment, the tower rewards you with a heavenly panorama of Barcelona.

▸ *Park Güell is free and open daily 10:00-20:00 (tel. 932-130-488). The semi-interesting Gaudí House Museum costs €5.50 and the skippable La Casa del Guarda is €2.*

The park is 2.5 miles north of Plaça de Catalunya. It's easiest to take a taxi to the main entrance (about €12). From Plaça de Catalunya, the blue Tourist Bus or public bus #24 travel to the park's side entrance.

Tibidabo

Barcelona's highest peak (1,600 feet), located five miles northwest of downtown, is topped with the city's oldest funfair (pricey but great for kids, www.tibidabo.cat), the Neo-Gothic Sacred Heart Church, and—if the weather and air quality are good—an almost limitless view of the city and the Mediterranean.

▸ *Get there by Metro, taxi, or the blue Tourist Bus. From the Tibidabo Metro station, catch a tram (the Tramvía Blau) to Plaça Dr. Andreu (€4.70 round-trip), then take a funicular to the top (€7.50).*

Day Trips

Three sights are day-trip temptations from Barcelona.

Figueres: Two hours by train from Barcelona, the town of Figueres (feeg-YEHR-ehs) is only of interest for its world-class Dalí Theater-Museum. It's an outrageously fun collection of work by the town's native son, the master Surrealist Salvador Dalí (1904-1989). True Dalí fans will continue another hour north of Figueres by bus to the sleepy fishing village of Cadaqués to visit the artist's family cabin, called the Salvador Dalí House.

▸ *Getting There: Trains to Figueres depart every 2 hours from Barcelona's Sants Station or from the RENFE station at Metro: Passeig de Gràcia (€15 express).*

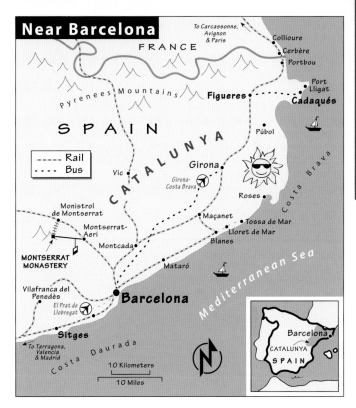

Near Barcelona

To Carcassonne, Avignon & Paris

Collioure

Cerbère

Portbou

Port Lligat

FRANCE

Pyrenees Mountains

Figueres

Cadaqués

S P A I N

Púbol

---- Rail
···· Bus

Vic

Girona

Girona-Costa Brava

C A T A L U N Y A

Roses

Costa Brava

Monistrol de Montserrat

Maçanet

Montserrat-Aeri

Tossa de Mar

Montcada

Lloret de Mar

Blanes

MONTSERRAT MONASTERY

Mataró

Mediterranean Sea

Vilafranca del Penedès

El Prat de Llobregat

Barcelona

Sitges

To Tarragona, Valencia & Madrid

Costa Daurada

10 Kilometers

10 Miles

N

Barcelona

CATALUNYA

SPAIN

The Dalí Theater-Museum (Teatre-Museu Dalí) in Figueres (€12) is open July-Sept daily 9:00-20:00; shorter hours and closed Mon off-season; last entry 45 minutes before closing. Tel. 972-677-500, www .salvador-dali.org.

The Salvador Dalí House in Cadaqués (€11) requires an advance reservation. Tel. 972-251-015, www.salvador-dali.org.

Sitges: For the consummate day at the beach, head 45 minutes south of Barcelona to this charming, artsy, and free-spirited resort town.

Today's Sitges (see-juhz) is a world-renowned vacation destination among the gay community. With a pleasant Old Town and fine beaches, it's a great break from the big city.

▶ *Getting There: From Barcelona's Sants Station or the Passeig de Gràcia RENFE station, take the Rodalies train on the dark-green line R2 toward Sant Vincenç de Calders (€8 round-trip).*

Montserrat: The "serrated mountain" rockets dramatically up from the valley floor northwest of Barcelona. With its unique rock formations, a dramatic mountaintop monastery (also called Montserrat), and spiritual connection with the Catalan people and their struggles, it's a popular day trip (tour groups mob the place at midday and on Sundays). You can see the Sacred Cave (where, in medieval times, some shepherd children found a Black Virgin statue), visit the Basilica (where the statue is venerated to-day), wander meditative trails, and stop into a small museum of sacred art.

▶ *Getting There: From Barcelona's Plaça d'Espanya (the FGC underground station), take train line R5 (1 hour, direction: Manresa) to the Montserrat-Aeri station at base of the mountain, where you can catch the scenic cable car (closed during lunchtime, www.aeridemontserrat .com). You can pay as you go or—smarter—buy combo-tickets (at Plaça de Catalunya TI or Plaça de Espanya train station) that cover the train, cable car, and admission to sights (packages range from €25-40).*

Sleeping

I favor hotels that are close to the sightseeing action: near Plaça de Catalunya, the Ramblas, the Barri Gòtic, and the Eixample.

I like places that are clean, small, central, quiet at night (except for the buzz of the neighborhood), traditional, inexpensive, family-run, friendly, and not listed in other guidebooks. A hotel with six out of these nine attributes is a keeper.

Double rooms listed in this book average around €125 (including a private bathroom), ranging from a low of roughly €60 (very simple, with toilet and shower down the hall) to €300 (modern rooms and chandeliered lobbies).

Although Spain has some of Western Europe's best hotel rates, Barcelona is Spain's most expensive city. Book ahead and look for

Hotel Price Code

$$$ Most rooms are €150 or more.

$$ Most rooms between €100–150.

$ Most rooms €100 or less.

These rates are for a standard double room during high season. Prices listed generally include the 8 percent IVA hotel tax. Many hotels charge extra for breakfast.

discounts (see "Budget Tips," next page). Hotel prices can fluctuate wildly from day-to-day and season-to season. It's hard to list firm prices—I've aimed for an average price. On the plus side, bargain-hunters can find some great deals.

A Typical Barcelona Hotel

A €125 double room in Barcelona is small by American standards and has one double bed or two twins. There's probably a bathroom in the room with a toilet, sink, and bathtub or shower. Rooms generally have a telephone and TV, and may have a safe. Most hotels at this price will have elevators and air-conditioning—cheaper places may not. (Travelers in spring and fall should prepare for hoteliers who may be stingy turning on the heat or air-conditioning.) Some rooms have a small fridge stocked with drinks for sale.

Breakfast is generally offered for an additional €5-15. It can range from a simple roll and coffee to a self-service buffet of cereal, ham, cheese, yogurt, and juice.

The hotel will likely have some form of Internet access, either free or pay-as-you-go. It may be Wi-Fi in your room or a public terminal in the lobby. The staff speaks at least enough English to get by. Night clerks aren't paid enough to care deeply about problems that arise. If you have issues, ask to see the complaint book *(libro de reclamaciones);* the request alone will generally prompt the hotelier to solve your problem. Hoteliers can be a great source of advice for everything from public transit and airport connections to finding a good restaurant or nearby launderette.

Since Barcelona parties late, street noise can be a problem, especially in cheap places with single-pane windows. You may have to choose between an atmospheric room with a view *(con vista)* or a quiet room in back *(tranquilo)*.

Making Hotel Reservations

Barcelona is the rare big city that doesn't empty out in summer, with high season *(temporada alta)* extending from July to September. Shoulder season *(temporada media)* is roughly April through June and October. Low season *(temporada baja)* runs from November through March. Barcelona's many festivals raise rates to peak-season levels.

Reserve your room by email (the best way), phone, fax, or through the hotel's website. Your hotelier will want to know:

- the type of room you want (e.g., "one double room with bath")

- how many nights ("three nights")

- dates (using European format: "arriving 22/7/13, departing 25/7/13")

- any special requests ("with twin beds, air-conditioning, quiet, view").

If the hotel requires your credit-card number for a deposit, you can send it by email (I do), but it's safer via phone, fax, or the hotel's secure website. Once your room is booked, print out the confirmation, and reconfirm your reservation with a phone call or email a day or two in advance. If you must cancel your reservation, hotels require advance notice or you'll be billed. Even if there's no penalty, it's polite to give at least three days' notice.

Budget Tips

Some of my listed hotels offer special rates to my readers—it's worth asking when you reserve your room.

As mentioned earlier, Barcelona hotel rates can change from day to day. To get the best deals, comparison shop. Email hotels directly (not through booking services) to ask for their best price. Check hotel websites for promo deals, then check again a few days later. You may get a better rate if you offer to pay cash, stay at least three nights, skip breakfast, or simply ask if there are any cheaper rooms. During festivals, rates can be sky-high. But rates can drop off-season—roughly November through March.

Big expensive hotels are most apt to mark down rooms. You might snag a €200 double for €100 by booking through a big hotel's website. At these business-class places, discounts are most likely—surprisingly—on weekends and in summer. (Conversely, less-expensive hotels are usually most crowded on weekends and in summer.) Given the economic downturn, hoteliers are eager to deal rather than let a room go empty.

In addition to hotels, I also list budget alternatives. The words *hostal* and *pension* designate cheap family-owned hotels. These may not have plush lobbies and modern amenities, but you'll get a fully private hotel room. I also recommend a few hostels *(albergue juvenil)*, where you can rent a dorm-style bed for around €25. For more hostel listings, try www.hostelz.com, www.hostelseurope.com, or Barcelona's excellent Equity Point Hostels (tel. 932-312-045, www.equity-point.com).

Renting an apartment can be a good value (around €100/day) for those who stay a week and do their own cooking. Find listings at the catch-all website www.homeaway.com, or with these two Barcelona companies: Cross-Pollinate (US tel. 800-270-1190, www.cross-pollinate.com, info@cross-pollinate.com) and Tournights Barcelona (mobile 620-585-594, www.tournights.com, info@tournights.com).

Don't be too cheap when picking a hotel in Barcelona. In this big, bustling, 24/7 city, it's nice to have a pleasant oasis to call home.

609.30

	Price	
NEAR PLAÇA DE CATALUNYA—Convenient location, plush lobbies, air-con, elevators, sterile modern rooms, and fluctuating prices—I've listed the average but always ask for a deal, especially on weekends and in summer		
Hotel Catalonia Plaça Catalunya	$$$	Four-star elegance, posh lobby, garden courtyard, comfortable but simple rooms, a world away from big-city noise
Hotel Denit	$$	36-room hotel on pedestrian street; chic, minimalist and fun; rooms priced by size (small, XL, etc.)
Hotel Inglaterra	$$	60 rooms, rooftop terrace and swimming pool, €15 breakfast
Hotel Reding	$$	10-minute walk west of Plaça, on quiet street, sleek place with 44 mod rooms at reasonable price
Hotel Lleó	$$	The "YEH-oh" is well-run with 92 big bright comfortable rooms, good public spaces, small rooftop pool
Hotel Atlantis	$$	50 big nondescript modern rooms, fair price for the location, on busy street—request quiet room in back, free Internet access and Wi-Fi
ON OR NEAR THE RAMBLAS—Generally family-run, with ad-lib furnishings, more character, and lower prices		
Hotel Continental Barcelona	$$	Tiny-balcony rooms with Ramblas views and noise, quieter back rooms, comfortable but faded, free snacks
Hostería Grau	$	Homey, cheery and family-run; garden-pastel rooms, away from Ramblas in colorful university district, strict cancellation policy
Hostal el Jardí	$	Clean, tight, and plain rooms; petite view balconies, you're paying for ambience of quaint Barri Gòtic square, book early
Hostal Operaramblas	$	Just off Ramblas, stark clean institutional modern rooms, semi-seedy at night but safe, great value

Handwritten annotations: "Maybe" near Hotel Denit with "15€/44", "300" near Hotel Inglaterra, "NO" near Hotel Reding, "NO" near Hotel Lleó, "Maybe" near Hotel Atlantis.

Sleeping

Address/Phone/Website/Email

Carrer de Bergara 11, Metro: Catalunya, tel. 933-015-151, fax 933-173-442, www.hoteles-catalonia.com, catalunya@hoteles-catalonia.es

Carrer d'Estruc 24-26, Metro: Catalunya, tel. 935-454-000, fax 935-454-001, www.denit.com, info@denit.com

Carrer de Pelai 14, Metro: Universitat, tel. 935-051-100, www.hotel-inglaterra.com, recepcion@hotel-inglaterra.com

Carrer de Gravina 5-7, Metro: Universitat, tel. 934-121-097, fax 932-683-482, www.hotelreding.com, recepcion@hotelreding.com

Carrer de Pelai 22, midway between Metros: Universitat and Catalunya, tel. 933-181-312, fax 934-122-657, www.hotel-lleo.com, info@hotel-lleo.com

Carrer de Pelai 20, midway between Metros: Universitat and Catalunya, tel. 933-189-012, fax 934-120-914, www.hotelatlantis-bcn.com, inf@hotelatlantis-bcn.com

Ramblas 138, Metro: Catalunya, tel. 933-012-570, fax 933-027-360, www.hotelcontinental.com, barcelona@hotelcontinental.com

200 yards up Carrer dels Tallers from the Ramblas at Ramelleres 27, Metro: Catalunya, tel. 933-018-135, fax 933-176-825, www.hostalgrau.com, reservas@hostalgrau.com, Monica

Halfway between Ramblas and cathedral at Plaça Sant Josep Oriol 1, Metro: Liceu, tel. 933-015-900, fax 933-425-733, www.eljardi-barcelona.com, reservations@eljardi-barcelona.com

Carrer de Sant Pau 20, Metro: Liceu, tel. 933-188-201, www.operaramblas.com, info@operaramblas.com

Sleeping

	Price	
IN THE OLD CITY—Buried in an atmospheric, tight tangle of lanes bordered by three Metro stops		
Hotel Neri	$$$	Posh, pretentious, and sophisticated; on small square near cathedral, flatscreen TVs, modern art, dressed-up staff
Hotel Nouvel	$$$	Victorian-style building with character on handy pedestrian street, royal lounges and 78 comfy rooms
NH Hotel Barcelona Centro	$$$	156-room chain hotel, predictably professional yet friendly, three blocks off Ramblas
Hotel Banys Orientals	$$	Modern business-class comfort with people-to-people ethic, on pedestrian street in El Born
Hotel Racó del Pi	$$	Chain hotel on colorful Barri Gòtic lane, big lobby, bright quiet modern rooms
Hotel Regencia Colón	$$	One block from cathedral, 50 older but solid, classy, and well-priced rooms
Hotel Cortés	$	Sterile and scruffy but good location, rooms face either quiet cloister or bustling shopping street
Hostal Campi	$	Big, ramshackle, and easygoing; simple with old-school class near top of Ramblas, no elevator
Gothic Point Hostel	$	130 dorm-style beds near Picasso Museum, roof terrace

137.92/no C [handwritten note]

Address/Phone/Website/Email

Carrer de Sant Sever 5, Metro: Liceu or Jaume I, tel. 933-040-655, fax 933-040-337, www.hotelneri.com, info@hotelneri.com

Carrer de Santa Anna 20, Metro: Catalunya, tel. 933-018-274, fax 933-018-370, www.hotelnouvel.com, info@hotelnouvel.com

Carrer del Duc 15, Metro: Catalunya or Liceu, tel. 932-703-410, fax 934-127-747, www.nh-hotels.com, barcelonacentro@nh-hotels.com

Between the cathedral and Church of Santa Maria del Mar at Carrer de l'Argenteria 37, 50 yards from Metro: Jaume I, tel. 932-688-460, www.hotelbanysorientals.com, reservas@hotelbanysorientals.com

Around the corner from Plaça del Pi at Carrer del Pi 7, 3-minute walk from Metro: Liceu, tel. 933-426-190, www.h10hotels.com, h10.raco.delpi@h10.es

Carrer dels Sagristans 13-17, Metro: Jaume I, tel. 933-189-858, fax 933-172-822, www.hotelregenciacolon.com, info@hotelregenciacolon.com

Between Plaça de Catalunya and cathedral at Carrer de Santa Anna 25, Metro: Catalunya, tel. 933-179-112, www.hotelcortes.com, reservas@hotelcortes.com

Carrer de la Canuda 4, Metro: Catalunya, tel. & fax 933-013-545, www.hostalcampi.com, reservas@hostalcampi.com, Margarita and Nando

Carrer Vigatans 5, Metro: Jaume I, reception tel. 932-687-808, www.gothicpoint.com

	Price		
IN THE EIXAMPLE—Uptown, boulevard-like neighborhood; 10-minute walk to the Ramblas			
Hotel Granvía	$$	Mansion with spacious rooms, plush lobby, peaceful sun patio, sometimes quirky service, some street noise	
Hotel Continental Palacete	$$	19 small rooms in mansion with flowery wallpaper; friendly, quiet, and well-located; outdoor terrace, free buffet	
Hotel Ginebra	$	Small and family-run, old building overlooking Placa de Catlunya, minimal and clean, choose views or quiet	
Hostal Oliva	$	Spartan old-school place in classic old building, 15 basic rooms, no breakfast or lobby, good location	
BCN Fashion House B&B	$	Small meditative place, peaceful lounge, leafy backyard terrace, in nondescript old building	
Centric Point Hostel	$	Huge place renting 400 cheap dorm beds in upscale location	
Somnio Hostel	$	Small, innovative American-run place with dorm beds and some private doubles	

Address/Phone/Website/Email

Gran Via de les Corts Catalanes 642, Metro: Catalunya, tel. 933-181-900, fax 933-189-997, www.hotelgranvia.com, hgranvia@nnhotels.com

2 blocks north of Plaça de Catalunya at 30 Rambla de Catalunya, Metro: Passeig de Gràcia, tel. 934-457-657, fax 934-450-050, www.hotelcontinental.com, palacete@hotelcontinental.com

Rambla de Catalunya 1/3, third floor, Metro: Catalunya, tel. 933-171-063, www.hotelginebra.net, info@hotelginebra.net

A couple of blocks above Plaça de Catalunya at Passeig de Gràcia 32, Metro: Passeig de Gràcia, tel. 934-880-162, www.hostaloliva.com, hostaloliva@lasguias.com

Carrer del Bruc 13, just steps from Metro: Urquinaona, mobile 637-904-044, www.bcnfashionhouse.com, info@bcnfashionhouse.com

Passeig de Gràcia 33, Metro: Passeig de Gràcia, tel. 932-151-796, fax 932-461-552, www.centricpointhostel.com

Carrer de la Diputació 251, second floor, Metro: Passeig de Gràcia, tel. 932-725-308, www.somniohostels.com, info@somniohostels.com

Eating

Barcelona is the capital of Catalan cuisine, starring fresh-caught seafood and a wide variety of tapas. Elbowing up to a lively bar for appetizers, then lingering over a late meal in a trendy bistro... they're some of Barcelona's great pleasures.

In general, Barcelona's restaurants rise to a higher level than elsewhere in Spain, propelled by cutting-edge chefs. But for many, Barcelona's real thrill is the tapas scene. At night, the city buzzes with people roaming the streets, popping into bars for a snack and a drink with friends.

I list a full range of restaurants and eateries—from everyman bars to chic splurges with maximum ambience. In fact, many fall somewhere in between a restaurant and bar, serving both stand-up tapas and sit-down meals. My recommendations are near the Ramblas (working-class places amid the tourists), the Barri Gòtic (atmospheric lanes and squares), the El Born (with the trendy bistros), and the modern, upscale Eixample.

Restaurant Price Rankings

$$$ Most main courses €15 or more.

$$ Most main courses €10-15.

$ Most main courses €10 or less.

Based on the average price of a meat or seafood dish (a main dish) on the menu. For tapas places, I've used the price of a *racion*. So a typical meal in a $$ restaurant—including appetizer, main dish, house wine, water, and service charge—would cost about €30. The circled numbers in the restaurant listings indicate locations on the maps on pages 162-165.

Eating on the Spanish Schedule

When in Barcelona, I eat on the local schedule. Breakfast (at the hotel or a corner bar) is little more than a roll and coffee. Around 11:00, many Spaniards grab a quick sandwich to tide them over. Lunch *(comida)*, around 14:00, is the major meal of the day, a social event enjoyed with friends and family. Dinner *(cena)* is light and eaten very late—after 21:00. At any time of day, Spaniards snack by popping into casual bars for tapas and drinks.

Restaurants

Restaurants generally serve lunch from 13:00 to 16:00 and dinner from 20:00 or even later. Don't expect a cheery "My name is Carlos and I'll be your waiter tonight." Service is professional, serious, and white-shirt-and-bow-tie proficient.

A full restaurant meal comes in courses, which can add up quickly if you order a la carte. For a budget meal, try a *plato combinado* (combination plate), which includes a main dish, vegetable, and bread for a reasonable price. Or try the *menú del día* (menu of the day, also known as *menú turístico*), a multi-course meal for a single price. Many of my recommended restaurants offer some kind of good-value fixed-price deal, especially at lunchtime.

If you order a la carte, main courses of meat or fish do not typically come with a side dish or vegetables. To get vegetables in your diet (always a challenge in Spain), concentrate on the first course selections—salads, vegetable soups, or sautéed vegetables.

Some restaurants don't have "starters" and "main dishes." Instead, they serve plate-size portions of tapas called *raciones*, or the smaller half-servings, *media-raciones*. A couple can build a great meal sharing four or five different *media-raciones*. It's economical (around €15/person) and lets you sample the cuisine.

All eateries in Spain are non-smoking. Many restaurants close for vacation in August. To get the bill, mime-scribble on your raised palm or ask: *"La cuenta?"* ✪ For hints on tipping, see page 172.

Bars, Cafés, and Other Budget Options

Spanish "bars" are not just taverns. These neighborhood hangouts serve coffee, croissants, sandwiches, *jamón*, fresh squeezed orange juice, light foods, and drinks (alcoholic and non). Some specialize in tapas, serving build-a-meal toothpick snacks for the local crowd.

At any eating establishment (however humble), be aware that there may be a three-tier price system. It's cheapest if you sit or stand at the counter *(barra)*. You may pay around 20 percent more to eat sitting at a table *(mesa* or *salón)* and another 20 percent for an outdoor table *(terraza)*. Prices are always clearly posted—don't sit without first checking out the financial consequences. (If you order food at the bar and then take it to a table, you may be charged the table price.) But in the right circumstances, a quiet snack and drink on a terrace can be well worth the extra charge. In bars and cafés, you pay at the end—your bartender is keeping track.

Besides restaurants and bar/cafés, there are eateries that fall somewhere in between. In these places, you can enjoy bite-size tapas at the bar, but if you sit you'll need to order large-portion *raciones*. The distinction can be blurry—observe, and follow the lead of locals.

Sandwich shops are everywhere, serving made-to-order *bocadillos*. Choose between bright (sterile) chain stores such as Bocatta and Pans & Company, or colorful holes-in-the-wall. Kebab places are another standby for quick and tasty €3-4 meals.

Picnickers can buy groceries at the basement supermarket in El Corte Inglés department store on Plaça de Catalunya, or at La Boqueria Market on the Ramblas (✪ see page 25). For a one-person picnic, I buy 100 grams *(cien gramos)* of super-high-quality *jamón ibérico extra* (your portion will run about €7), 100 grams of chorizo (spicy sausage), 50 grams of manchego cheese, and some olives and pickles. Add some red wine and dine like a duke.

Survival Tips

If you're hungry outside of Barcelona's traditional mealtimes, do as the locals do and feast on bar food. Although some bars have a dizzying array of fancy tapas, even humble establishments will likely have some of these items:

Bocadillo—A sandwich on baguette bread. The most popular is a *bocadillo de jamón* (ham).

Café con leche—Coffee with hot milk

Zumo de naranja natural—Fresh-squeezed orange juice

Tortilla española—A very thick potato omelet, served either hot or cold

Ensaladilla rusa—Salad of potatoes and vegetables in mayonnaise

Patatas bravas—Fried potatoes with spicy ketchup

Jamón—Thin-sliced ham on a plate

Queso manchego—Sheeps' milk cheese from La Mancha

Pimientos de Padrón—Fried green peppers, mostly mild but with the occasional Russian-roulette hot one

Tapas Bars

Tapas bars are a big part of the Barcelona scene. Locals stop in at lunch, early evening, or late at night for a drink and to snack on various finger foods—tapas. Throughout the city, you'll see signs for *tascas* (tapas bars), *tapas*, and *tapes* (the Catalan word for tapas, same pronunciation).

Choices range from cheese to olives to deep-fried croquettes to calamari rings to meatballs to ugly seafood on a toothpick. Just belly up to the bar, point to the tapas you want (sometimes displayed on trays), and eat. It's easy to build a €10 meal out of small €2-3 servings. Tapas come in various portions. A "*pincho*" is bite-size; a "*tapa*" is snack-size. For €8-10, you can get still larger portions, either a dinner-plate-size *racion* or a small-plate-size *media racion*. An assortment plate *(surtido)* lets you sample various meats, cheeses, or whatever. Be aware that most bars try to push the larger portions *(raciones)*, and some simply won't sell anything less than a full *racion*, especially if you sit at a table.

The system is simple, but frankly, ordering in a crowded bar and dealing with a brusque bartender can be intimidating. Hang back and observe. When you're ready to order, be assertive—"*Por favor* (please)" grabs the guy's attention. Order a drink to start—*un caña* (draft beer) or *un tinto* (red wine). Then quickly rattle off what you'd like (pointing to other people's food if necessary). As you eat, follow the lead of locals and throw your dirty napkins on the floor.

Basque-style tapas places (signs say *Basca* or *Euskal*) are particularly user-friendly. You order a drink, help yourself from a buffet spread, and save your toothpicks—they'll count them up at the end to tally your bill.

A few tips: Although tapas are served all day, the real action begins after 21:00. But for beginners, an earlier start comes with less commotion. Chasing down a particular bar nearly defeats the purpose and spirit of tapas—they are impromptu. I look for noisy spots with the TV blaring a bullfight, soccer game, or silly game show (you'll see Vanna Blanco). Unlike in many Spanish cities, most Barcelona tapas bars do *not* provide a free, small tapa with the purchase of a drink. The cheapest seats are at the bar, and it comes with the best show. Study your bartender—he's an artist.

Signature Dishes

The Spanish diet is heavy on *jamón* and deep-fried foods. The Catalan influence adds seafood, rice dishes, and the flavorings of garlic and olive oil.

For starters, try *pa amb tomàquet* (pah ahm too-MAH-kaht)—toasted bread with tomato paste, served alone or to accompany other appetizers. The classic Spanish appetizer is *jamón* (hah-MOHN)—prosciutto-like ham that's dry-cured and aged. It's generally sliced thin and served raw on a plate. Bars proudly hang ham hocks from the rafters as part of the decor. Like connoisseurs of fine wine, Spaniards rhapsodize about their favorite ham: *Jamón serrano* comes from white pigs from the sierras (mountains). The higher-quality *jamón ibérico* is made with the back legs of black-hooved, pampered pigs.

For main dishes in this port town, seafood is king—cod, hake, tuna, squid, and anchovies. Other popular dishes include *fideuà* (a thin, flavor-infused noodle served with seafood) and *arròs negre* (black rice in squid ink). Spaniards don't tend to eat as many vegetables as Americans, but you will find salads and sautéed vegetables on the appetizers menu.

In Spain, dessert is often an afterthought—some fruit, cheese, flan, or ice cream. Catalunya, however, is known for its *crema Catalana* (crème brulee). A popular Spanish treat, eaten late at night or for breakfast, is *churros*. These greasy cigar-shaped fritters are for dipping in warm chocolate pudding.

No Spanish meal is complete without a drink. Spain produces lots of excellent wines—red *(tinto)* and white *(blanco)*. Catalunya's wine regions include Valdepeñas and Penedès, producing mostly Cabernet-style wines. For a basic glass of red house wine, order *un tinto*. But ordering *un crianza* (aged) can give you a significantly higher-quality wine for only a little more money. Other popular wine drinks are *cava* (Spanish champagne), *tinto de varano* (wine with lemonade), and *jerez* (dry sherry, not the sweet dessert variety).

If you order a *caña* (small draft beer), you'll likely get one of the locally brewed lagers, Estrella Damm, Moritz, or San Miguel. A *clara con limón* is a small beer with lemonade. Nonalcoholic beer *("una sin")* is quite popular, as is nonalcoholic wine *(mosto)*. *Orxata* (or *horchata*) is a milky, nonalcoholic beverage made from chufa nuts.

Salud!

Eating

	Price		
RAMBLAS NEIGHBORHOOD—Handy, no-nonsense places amid the tourist bustle (see map, pages 162-163)			
❶ Taverna Basca Irati	$	Fun user-friendly tapas bar, wide variety of Basque *pintxos,* grab what you like, count up toothpicks and pay at the end	
❷ Restaurant Elisabets	$	Rough popular local eatery, €12 lunch special served daily 13:00-16:00, otherwise tapas only, indifferent service	
❸ Café Granja Viader	$	Quaint family-run feminine-feeling place, baked goods, sandwiches, traditional breakfast, dairy-based sweets, *orxata*	
❹ La Boqueria Market	$	Picnic-shopper's paradise for fresh produce, take-away food, people-watching, and cheap colorful eateries	
❹ Pinotxo Bar	$	Grab a stool for coffee, breakfast, tapas, and people-watching; fun-loving owner, don't overspend	
❹ Kiosko Universal	$	Line up for great-value fresh-caught fish dishes amid market action, €14 fixed-price lunch	
❺ Restaurant la Gardunya	$$	Ultra-fresh meat and seafood meals, €14 fixed-price lunch or €17 dinner or à la carte, mod seating indoors or outside in market	
❻ Biocenter	$	Vegetarian soup-and-salad restaurant, serious about food, €8-10 weekday lunch specials, €15 dinner	
❼ Juicy Jones	$	Vegan/vegetarian food and many fresh-squeezed juices, colorful graffiti decor, hip menu and staff, €6-10 lunch meals	

Operating Hours and Days	Address/Phone
Daily 11:00-24:00	A block off the Ramblas, behind arcade at Carrer del Cardenal Casanyes 17, Metro: Liceu, tel. 933-023-084
Mon-Sat 7:30-23:00, closed Sun and Aug	2 blocks west of Ramblas on far corner of Plaça del Bonsuccés at Carrer d'Elisabets 2, Metro: Catalunya, tel. 933-175-826
Tue-Sat 9:00-13:30 & 17:00-20:30, Mon 17:00-20:30 only, closed Sun	A block off the Ramblas behind Betlem Church at Xuclà 4, Metro: Liceu, tel. 933-183-486
Market open Mon-Sat 8:00-20:00, gets quiet after 16:00, closed Sun	Ramblas #91, Metro: Liceu
Mon-Sat 8:00-16:00, closed Sun	Just inside La Boqueria Market on the right-hand side, Metro: Liceu
Mon-Sat 12:00-16:00, closed Sun	As you enter La Boqueria Market, it's all the way to the left in the first alley; Metro: Liceu, tel. 933-178-286
Mon-Sat 13:00-16:00 & 20:00-24:00, closed Sun	Carrer Jerusalem 18, Metro: Liceu, tel. 933-024-323
Mon-Sat 13:00-23:00, Sun 13:00-16:00	2 blocks off the Ramblas at Carrer del Pintor Fortuny 25, Metro: Liceu, tel. 933-014-583
Daily 9:00-23:30	Carrer del Cardenal Casanyes 7, Metro: Liceu, tel. 933-024-330

Eating

Eating

	Price	
BARRI GÒTIC—Atmospheric neighborhood with sit-down restaurants (listed first) and tapas bars (see map, pages 162-163)		
8 Café de l'Academia	$$	Delightful place on mellow square, local crowd, "honest cuisine," candlelit soft-jazz interior or outside
9 Els Quatre Gats	$$$	"The Four Cats" fed Picasso and now feeds tourists (go after 21:00), still good food and service, not too overpriced, lunch special Mon-Fri 13:00-16:00
10 La Dolça Herminia	$$	Bright modern Adelana chain restaurant, great-value Catalan/Mediterranean food, no reservations, lines
11 Xaloc	$	Classic classy wood-paneled place, gourmet tapas and home-style meals, fun energy, good service and prices, top-notch *jamón*
12 Bar del Pi	$	Simple, hardworking bar for salads, sandwiches, and tapas; some outdoor tables on ultra-atmospheric little square
13 Restaurant Agut	$$	Since 1924, modern, sophisticated, slightly bohemian, art-lined walls, tasty Catalan food, €13 lunch deal
14 Les Quinze Nits	$$	Bright, modern, and wildly popular (long lines, no reservations); artfully presented Catalan and Mediterranean cuisine at unbeatable prices, part of Andelana chain (as are the next 2 listings)
15 La Crema Canela	$$	Also part of Andelana chain, similar to Les Quinze Nits but feels cozier and takes reservations
16 La Fonda	$$	Another Andelana place, so expect good food, prices, ambience, and lines to get in
17 Tapas Bars on Carrer de la Mercè	$	Street in rough-edged, unvarnished old Barcelona with many greasy-spoon tapas bars; hop from bar to bar, enjoying cheap sardines, clams, and octopus *(pulpo)*, all washed down with cider or €1 wine
18 Seafood Places in the Barceloneta Neighborhood	$$-$$$	Harborfront neighborhood facing the city has a number of classy if interchangeable seafood restaurants (try La Mar Salada)

Operating Hours and Days	Address/Phone
Mon-Fri 13:30-16:00 & 20:30-23:30, closed Sat-Sun	Near City Hall square, off Carrer de Jaume I up Carrer de la Dagueria at Carrer dels Lledó 1, Metro: Jaume I, tel. 933-198-253
Daily 10:00-24:00	Just steps off Avinguda del Portal de l'Angel at Carrer de Montsió 3, Metro: Catalunya, tel. 933-024-140
Daily 13:00-15:45 & 20:30-23:30	Near Palace of Catalan Music at Carrer de les Magdalenes 27, Metro: Jaume I, tel. 933-170-676
Daily	A block toward the cathedral from Plaça de Sant Josep Oriol at Carrer de la Palla 13, Metro: Catalunya, tel. 933-011-990
Tue-Sun 9:00-23:00, closed Mon	On Plaça de Sant Josep Oriol 1, Metro: Liceu, tel. 933-022-123
Tue-Sat 13:30-16:00 & 21:00-24:00, Sun 13:30-16:00 only, closed Mon	Just up from Carrer de la Mercè and the harbor at Carrer d'En Gignàs 16, Metro: Jaume I, tel. 933-151-709
Daily 11:00-16:30 & 19:00-23:00	Plaça Reial 6, near Metro: Liceu, tel. 933-173-075
Daily 13:00-15:45 & 20:00-23:30	A few steps north of Plaça Reial at Passatge de Madoz 6, Metro: Liceu, tel. 933-182-744
Daily 13:00-15:45 & 19:30-23:30	A block south of Plaça Reial at Carrer dels Escudellers 10, Metro: Liceu, tel. 933-017-515
Most places daily 11:00-23:00, but liveliest 19:00-22:00	From the bottom of the Ramblas (Metro: Drassanes), hike east along Carrer de Josep Anselm Clavé
La Mar Salada open Wed-Mon for lunch and dinner, closed Tue	From Metro: Barceloneta, head south along Passeig Joan de Borbó; La Mar Salada is at #58 (tel. 932-212-127)

Eating

Eating

	Price	
IN EL BORN, NEAR THE PICASSO MUSEUM—Trendy, eclectic, classy bistros for foodies in small-lane neighborhood (see map, page 163)		
⑲ **Bar del Pla**	$	Local favorite, classic diner/bar for tapas and traditional dishes, same price at bar or table but bar has best scene
⑳ **La Vinya del Senyor**	$$	Location on charming pedestrian square by church is its main asset, good wine list, ham-cheese-tapas menu
㉑ **El Senyor Parellada**	$$	Former cloister, now white-tablecloth restaurant w/smart, tourist-friendly staff, Catalan cuisine w/modern twist
㉒ **Sagardi Euskal Taberna**	$	Lavish Basque tapas array, count toothpicks to pay, 20 percent more to sit outside, try Txakolí wine
㉒ **Sagardi**	$$	Mod but rustic restaurant for high-quality Basque steaks and grilled specialties, sizzling-grill ambience, reservations smart
㉓ **Taller de Tapas**	$$$	Upscale and sophisticated place for tapas and light meals, medieval-meets-mod setting, a bit stuffy, build a meal for €20
㉔ **El Xampanyet**	$$	Colorful fun-loving family-run tapas bar specializing in anchovies, tourists by day and locals by night, same price at bar or table

Operating Hours and Days	Address/Phone
Tue-Sun 12:00-24:00, closed Mon	With your back to the Picasso Museum, head right 2 blocks, past Carrer de la Princesa, to Carrer de Montcada 2; Metro: Jaume I, tel. 932-683-003
Tue-Sun 12:00-24:00, closed Mon	Plaça de Santa Maria 5, Metro: Jaume I or Barceloneta, tel. 933-103-379
Daily	Carrer de l'Argenteria 37, 100 yards from Metro: Jaume I, tel. 933-105-094
Daily 12:00-24:00	Carrer de l'Argenteria 62-64, Metro: Jaume I, tel. 933-199-993
Daily 13:00-16:00 & 20:00-24:00	Part of the Sagardi tapas bar at Carrer de l'Argenteria 62, Metro: Jaume I, tel. 933-199-993
Daily 8:30-24:00	Carrer de l'Argenteria 51, Metro: Jaume I, tel. 932-688-559
Tue-Sat 12:00-15:30 & 19:00-23:00, Sun 12:00-16:00 only, closed Mon	A half-block beyond the Picasso Museum at Carrer de Montcada 22, Metro: Jaume I, tel. 933-197-003

Eating

Eating

	Price	
THE EIXAMPLE—People-packed boulevards lined with upscale restaurants and tapas bars featuring breezy outdoor seating (see map, pages 164-165)		
㉕ La Rita	$$	Fresh and dressy little restaurant for Catalan cuisine, great-value fixed-price lunches and dinners, no reservations, lines
㉖ La Bodegueta	$	Atmospheric wine cellar for tapas (anchovies), sandwiches *(flautas)*, and vermouth; outside tables, €12 lunch special
㉗ Restaurante la Palmera	$$	Catalan/French cuisine, untouristy, great food and service, bottle-lined main room is best, can be exceptional value, reservations smart
㉘ La Flauta	$	Fun, fresh, and modern; no-stress small-plate-and-sandwich menu, enthusiastic eaters, ground floor is best, let staff recommend
㉙ Cinc Sentits	$$$	30-seat chic and slightly snooty place for gourmets, fine service, beautifully presented avant-garde Catalan cuisine, fixed-price menus only, €60-80 buys unforgettable extravaganza, reservations required
㉚ Tapas 24	$$	Fun local tapas bar, same price inside or out, happy energy, top-notch tapas from famous chef Carles Abellan
㉛ Quasi Queviures ("Qu Qu")	$$	Upscale tapas or full meals, bright modern décor, high-energy ambience, pleasantly uncrowded with locals
㉜ Ciutat Comtal Cerveceria	$$	Classy tapas-only favorite brags about the best finger sandwiches *(montaditos)* and beers in Barcelona, eat inside or out
㉝ La Tramoia	$$	Another great *montaditos* and tapas place, plus OK brasserie-style restaurant for grilled meats

Operating Hours and Days	Address/Phone
Daily 13:00-15:45 & 20:00-23:30	Near corner of Carrer de d'Aragó at d'Aragó 279, Passeig de Gràcia, tel. 9
Mon-Sat 8:00-24:00, Sun 19:00-24:00	A long block from Gaud with Carrer de Provenç Metro: Provença, tel. 9
Mon-Sat 13:00-15:45 & 20:30-23:15, closed Sun	Carrer d'Enric Granados 57, at the corner with Carrer Mallorca, Metro: Provença, tel. 934-532-338
Mon-Sat 13:00-24:00, closed Sun	Just off Carrer de la Diputació at Carrer d'Aribau 23, Metro: Universitat, tel. 933-237-038
Tue-Sat 13:30-15:00 & 20:30-22:30, closed Sun-Mon	Near Carrer d'Aragó at Carrer d'Aribau 58, between Metros: Universitat and Provença, tel. 933-239-490, maître d' Amelia
Mon-Sat 9:00-24:00, closed Sun	Just off Passeig de Gràcia at Carrer de la Diputació 269, tel. 934-880-977
Mon-Sat 8:00-24:00, Sun 10:30-24:00	Between Gran Via de les Corts Catalanes and Carrer de la Diputació at Passeig de Gràcia 24, tel. 933-174-512
Daily 8:00-24:00, packed after 21:00	Facing the intersection of Gran Via de les Corts Catalanes and Rambla de Catalunya at Rambla de Catalunya 18, tel. 933-181-997
Daily 12:00-24:00 for tapas, 13:00-16:00 & 17:30-24:00 for meals	Across the street from Ciutat Comtal Verveceria at Rambla de Catalunya 15, tel. 934-123-634

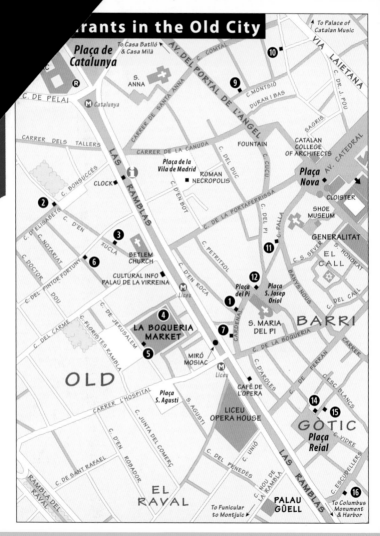

Plaça de Catalunya

To Palace of Catalan Music

To Casa Batlló & Casa Milà

VIA LAIETANA

AV. DEL PORTAL DE L'ANGEL

C. COMTAL

10

S. ANNA

C. DE PELAI

R

M Catalunya

C. MONTSIÓ

9

DURAN I BAS

C. DR. J. POU

CARRER DELS TALLERS

CARRER DE SANTA ANNA

SAGRIS

CARRER DE LA CANUDA

FOUNTAIN

CATALAN COLLEGE OF ARCHITECTS

C. BONSUCCÉS

CLOCK

Plaça de la Vila de Madrid

ROMAN NECROPOLIS

C. DEL DUC

C. CUCU

AV. CATEDRAL

Plaça Nova

LAS RAMBLAS

i

CLOISTER

2

C. D'ELISABEIG

C. D'EN

C. D'EN BOT

C. DE LA PORTAFERRISSA

C. DEL PI

C. PALLA

SHOE MUSEUM

C. NOTARIAT

XUCLÀ

3

BETLEM CHURCH

GENERALITAT

C. DOCTOR

6

C. PETRITXOL

11

C. S. SEVER

EL CALL

C. S. HONORAT

C. DEL PINTOR FORTUNY

CULTURAL INFO PALAU DE LA VIRREINA

C. D'EN ROCA

12

Plaça del Pi

Plaça S. Josep Oriol

BANYS NOUS

DOU

M Liceu

1

BARRI

C. DE JERUSALEM

4

CARDENA

S. MARIA DEL PI

C. DEL CALL

C. DEL CARME

C. FLORISTES RAMBLA

LA BOQUERIA MARKET

7

C. DE LA BOQUERIA

CARRER

5

MIRÓ MOSIAC

OLD

M Liceu

C. D'AROLES

C. DE FERRAN

C. ESC BLANCS

CARRER L'HOSPITAL

Plaça S. Agustí

S. AGUSTÍ

CAFÉ DE L'OPERA

14

GÒTIC

C. JUNTA DEL COMERÇ

15

LICEU OPERA HOUSE

Plaça Reial

C. VIDRE

C. D'EN ROBADOR

C. DEL PENEDÈS

C. D'EN

C. DEL UNIÓ

LAS RAMBLAS

C. ESCUDELLERS

RAMBLA DEL RAVAL

C. DE SANT RAFAEL

EL RAVAL

C. NOU DE LA RAMBLA

PALAU GÜELL

16

To Funicular to Montjuïc

To Columbus Monument & Harbor

Eating

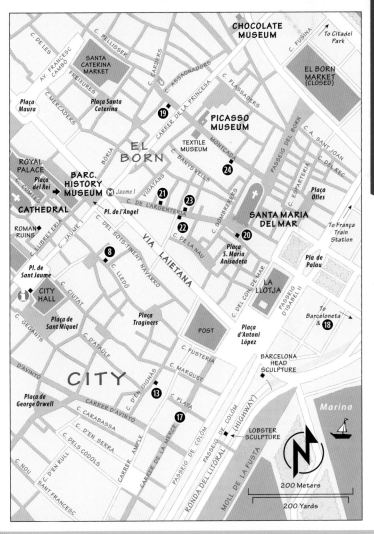

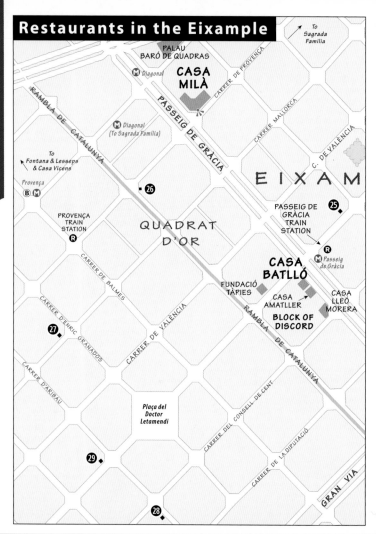

Restaurants in the Eixample

To Sagrada Familia

PALAU BARÓ DE QUADRAS

CASA MILÀ

M Diagonal

CARRER DE PROVENÇA

RAMBLA DE CATALUNYA

PASSEIG DE GRÀCIA

M Diagonal (To Sagrada Familia)

CARRER MALLORCA

To Fontana & Lesseps & Casa Vicens

C. DE VALÈNCIA

EIXAM

Provença
B M

26

QUADRAT D'OR

PASSEIG DE GRÀCIA TRAIN STATION

25

PROVENÇA TRAIN STATION
R

R Passeig de Gràcia

CASA BATLLÓ

FUNDACIÓ TÀPIES

CASA AMATLLER

CASA LLEÓ MORERA

CARRER DE BALMES

BLOCK OF DISCORD

CARRER D'ENRIC GRANADOS

27

CARRER DE VALÈNCIA

RAMBLA DE CATALUNYA

CARRER D'ARIBAU

Plaça del Doctor Letamendi

CARRER DEL CONSELL DE CENT

29

CARRER DE LA DIPUTACIÓ

GRAN VIA

28

Eating

To Hospital de la
Santa Creu i Sant Pau
& Bus #92
to Park Güell

CARRER D'ARAGÓ

LA
CONCEPCIÓ
MARKET

CHURCH
OF THE HOLY
CONCEPTION

200 Meters

200 Yards

CARRER DEL BRUC

CARRER DEL CONSELL DE CENT

Girona

Tetuan

PLE

CARRER DEL BAILEN

CARRER DE DIPUTACIÓ

PASSATGE MEDEZVIGO

C. DE ROGER DE LLÚRIA

TOWER

Water
Tower
Gardens

CARRER DE GIRONA

C. DE PAU CLARIS

PASSATGE PERMANYER

CARRER DEL BRUC

30

31

PASSEIG

CORTS CATALANES

CARRER DE CASP

CARRER D'AUSIÀS MARC

RONDA DE SANT PERE

Bus #50
to Montjuïc

CARRER DE PAU CLARIS

Urquinaona

DE LES

DE GRÀCIA

ZARA
STORE

Passeig de
Gràcia

C. DE LES JONQUERES

C. D'ORTIGOSA

Urquinaona

32

33

EL CORTE INGLÉS
DEPARTMENT
STORE

VIA LAIETANA

PALACE OF
CATALAN
MUSIC

Catalunya

Bus to Airport
(& Taxis)

C. FONTANELLA

Plaça de
Catalunya

OLD

CITY

Practicalities

PLANNING

When to Go

Sea breezes off the Mediterranean make Barcelona pleasant for much of the year. Late spring and early fall offer the best combination of good weather (in the low 70s), light crowds, long days, and plenty of tourist and cultural activities. July and August bring hot, humid weather (in the low 80s) and the biggest crowds, and some shops and restaurants close down in August. Winter temperatures are mild (mid-50s). Expect some rain one day a week throughout the year. Barcelona's many festivals throughout the year can bring especially big crowds and fill up hotels.

Before You Go

Make sure your passport is up to date (to renew, see www.travel.state .gov). Call your debit- and credit-card companies about your plans (see below). Book hotel rooms and make reservations for key sights, especially for travel during peak season or holiday weekends. Consider buying travel insurance (see www.ricksteves.com/insurance). If traveling beyond Barcelona, research transit schedules (trains, buses) and car rentals. Barcelona makes a good first or last stop on a Spain trip: It's easy to fly into Barcelona, then travel to Madrid on a 2.5-hour AVE train (www.renfe .com) or cheap flight (Vueling Air starts at €50, www.vueling.com).

MONEY

Spain uses the euro currency: 1 euro (€) = about $1.30. To convert prices in euros to dollars, add about 40 percent: €20 = about $26, €50 = about $65. (Check www.oanda.com for the latest exchange rates.)

Withdraw money from a cash machine using a debit card, just like at home. Visa and MasterCard are commonly used throughout Europe. Before departing, call your bank and credit-card company: Confirm that your card will work overseas, ask about international transaction fees, and alert them that you'll be making withdrawals in Europe. Many travelers bring a second (or third) debit/credit card as a backup.

While American credit cards are accepted almost everywhere in Europe, they will not work in some automated payment machines. Instead, pay with cash, try your PIN code (ask your credit-card company or use a

Helpful Websites

Spanish Tourist Information: www.spain.info
Barcelona Tourist Information: www.barcelonaturisme.cat
Other Helpful Barcelona Websites: www.barcelonaplanning.com,
www.guiadelocio.com/barcelona, and www.butxaca.com
Cheap Flights: www.kayak.com (international flights), www.sky
scanner.com (flights within Europe), or www.vueling.com (flights
within Spain).
European Train Schedules: www.bahn.com
General Travel Tips: www.ricksteves.com (trip planning, packing
lists, and more—plus updates for this book)

debit card), or find a nearby cashier, who should be able to process the transaction.

To keep your valuables safe, wear a money belt. But if you do lose your credit or debit card, report the loss immediately. Call these 24-hour US numbers collect: Visa (tel. 303/967-1096), MasterCard (tel. 636/722-7111), and American Express (tel. 336/393-1111).

ARRIVAL IN BARCELONA

I don't recommend driving in Barcelona. Even parking a car here is expensive. If you're renting a car for a Spain trip, it's better to do it in Madrid, and connect to Barcelona by train or air.

El Prat de Llobregat Airport

Barcelona's airport (airport code: BCN) is eight miles southwest of town. It has two large terminals, linked by shuttle buses. Most airlines use Terminal 1. Both terminals have the necessary services—TI, post office, pharmacy, a left-luggage office, eateries, and ATMs. (At Terminal 1, avoid the gimmicky ATM machines before the baggage carousels—use the bank-affiliated ATMs in the main arrivals hall.) Airport info: Tel. 913-211-000, www.aena -aeropuertos.es.

To get between the airport and downtown Barcelona, you have three options:

Taxi: A taxi for the 30-minute trip into town costs about €30—about €25 on the meter plus a €3.10 airport supplement and fee of €1 per bag.

Bus: The Aerobus leaves from immediately outside the arrivals lobby of both terminals (bus #A1 for Terminal 1 and #A2 for Terminal 2). In about 30 minutes you arrive at Plaça de Catalunya and other stops, including Plaça d'Espanya (departs every 5 minutes, from airport 6:00-1:00 in the morning, from downtown 5:30-24:15, €5.65 one-way, €9.75 round-trip, buy ticket from machine or from driver, tel. 934-156-020.)

Train: The RENFE train (on the Rodalies R2 Sud line) leaves from Terminal 2 only, heading to Sants Station, Passeig de Gràcia Station (near Plaça de Catalunya), and França Station (10-minute walk from Terminal 2 to the station—follow signs, departs 2/hour, €3 or covered by T10 Card).

Sants Train Station

Barcelona has several train stations, but virtually all trains (including the AVE from Madrid) end up at Sants, located west of the Old City. It's vast but manageable, with a TI, ATMs, shops, eateries, a classy Sala Club lounge for first-class travelers, and luggage storage (€5/day, near tracks 13-14). If you need train tickets (it's smart to reserve a day ahead in Spain), you can wait in line at the station, or use helpful travel agencies in many El Corte Inglés department stores. It's also possible by phone (902-240-202) or at www.renfe.com (undependable) or www.raileurope.com (service fee).

To get downtown, take the Metro L3 (green) line, which links to a number of useful points in town, including Plaça de Catalunya. Alternatively, you can take any Rodalies suburban train from track 8 (R1, R3, or R4) to Plaça de Catalunya.

Cruise Ship Ports

Most American cruise lines put in at Moll Adossat/Muelle Adosado, beneath Montjuïc, two miles from the bottom of the Ramblas. For the trip into town, taxis are always waiting—it's about €10 to the Ramblas and €15 to Plaça de Catalunya. Or you can take a shuttle bus to the bottom of the Ramblas (follow *Public Bus* signs to *lanzadera*, #T3, €3 round-trip, tel. 932-986-000).

HELPFUL HINTS

Tourist Information (TI): Barcelona's TI has several branches. The central contact number is tel. 932-853-834 (www.barcelonaturisme.cat).

The main TI is at Plaça de Catalunya, along the southeast side of the square, across from the Hard Rock Café—look for the red sign (daily 8:30-20:30, tel. 932-853-832). Other convenient branches in the Old City are near the top of the Ramblas at #115 (mobile 618-783-479), on Plaça de Sant Jaume, and at the Columbus Monument. In the Eixample neighborhood, the Catalunya TI gives tips on Barcelona and the entire region, with special emphasis (and discounts) on Modernista sights (Passeig de Gràcia 107, tel. 932-388-091, www.catalunya.com). There are TIs at the airport and at Sants train station. Besides these major TIs, helpful kiosks (and young, red-jacketed helpers) often spring up in touristy locales.

At any TI, pick up the free city map (although the free Corte Inglés map provided by most hotels is better), the small Metro map, and various free periodicals with sightseeing tips, shopping, events, and restaurants.

TIs are handy places to buy tickets for the hop-on hop-off Tourist Bus (described later) or for the TI-run walking tours (described later). Most TIs also provide a room-booking service.

Hurdling the Language Barrier: Many Barcelonans prefer the Catalan language, though everyone also speaks Spanish *(castellano)*. Signs almost always list both. Most people in the tourist industry—and virtually all young people—speak at least a little English. Get a start learning a little Catalan and Spanish with the survival phrases on pages 187-190.

Time Zones: Spain's time zone is generally six/nine hours ahead of the East/West Coasts of the US.

Watt's Up? Europe's electrical system is 220 volts, instead of North America's 110 volts. Most newer electronics (including hair dryers, laptops, and battery chargers) convert automatically, so you won't need a voltage converter—but you will need a special adapter plug with two round prongs, sold inexpensively at US and Canadian travel stores.

Numbers and Stumblers: What Americans call the second floor of a building is the first floor in Europe. Europeans write dates as day/month/year, so Christmas is 25/12/13. Commas are decimal points and vice versa—a dollar and a half is 1,50, and there are 5.280 feet in a mile.

Spain uses the metric system: A kilogram is 2.2 pounds; a liter is about a quart; and a kilometer is six-tenths of a mile. Temperature is

Tipping

Spaniards rarely tip, so tipping in Spain isn't as automatic and generous as it is in the US. At Spanish restaurants that have waitstaff, a 10-15 percent service charge is generally included in the bill's grand total. Spaniards don't tip beyond this, but if the service is exceptional, you can round up by as much as 5 percent. At hotels, you could give porters a euro for each bag, and tip the maid by leaving a euro per night at the end of your stay—but neither is expected. To tip a taxi driver, round up to the nearest euro (for a €5.50 fare, give €6), or up to 10 percent for longer rides.

measured in Celsius. 0°C = 32°F. To convert Celsius to Fahrenheit, double the number and add 30.

Holidays: Many sights and banks close down on national holidays. Barcelona celebrates more local festivals than most places. Verify dates at www.barcelonaturisme.cat, or check www.ricksteves.com/festivals.

Business Hours: Many businesses respect the afternoon siesta, when locals break for their main meal and get out of the afternoon heat. Shops are generally open Monday through Saturday 10:00-13:00 and 16:00-20:00, though some shops may not be open Saturday evenings. Tourist-friendly shops are often open on Sunday. Banking hours are generally Monday through Friday 9:00-14:00.

Laundry: Several self-service launderettes (€7/load) are located around the Old City. Wash 'n Dry is a block west of the Ramblas, near Palau Güell, at Carrer Nou de la Rambla 19 (daily 9:00-23:00, tel. 934-121-953). Laundromat Pasaje Elisabets is near Plaça de Catalunya at Passatge Elisabets 3 (daily 8:00-22:00, tel. 933-026-607).

Services: Public WCs are scarce. Use them when you can, in any café or museum you patronize.

GETTING AROUND BARCELONA

Barcelona is big enough that, at some point, you will need to take public transportation. The Old City (Ramblas and Barri Gòtic) is great for walking. But taxis and the Metro make the rest of the city easily accessible.

By Metro

Barcelona's Metro (www.tmb.cat) is among Europe's best, connecting just about every place you'll visit. An individual ticket (€2) covers 1.25 hours of unlimited use (including transfers) on the Metro, bus, and several suburban train lines. The T10 Card is a great deal—€9.25 gives you 10 rides, cutting the per-ride cost more than in half. Travel companions can share a T10 Card. All-day passes are also available (1 day-€7, 5 days-up to €27). Buy tickets and passes from machines (with English instructions) at Metro entrances. These machines can be temperamental about accepting bills, so try to have change on hand.

The Metro works like most any transit system. Find signs for your line number—for example, the "L3." Then find the L3 train headed the direction you're going (e.g., "L3 - Trinitata Nova"). Insert your ticket into the turnstile (with the arrow pointing in), then reclaim it. Keep your bags close by and beware pickpockets.

The most useful line for tourists is the L3 (green). Handy stops include (in order):

Sants Estació—Main train station

Espanya—Plaça d'Espanya, at the bottom of Montjuïc

Paral-lel—Funicular to the top of Montjuïc

Drassanes—Bottom of the Ramblas, near Maritime Museum and Maremagnum mall

Liceu—Middle of the Ramblas, near the heart of the Barri Gòtic and cathedral

Plaça de Catalunya—Top of the Ramblas and main square with TI, airport bus, and lots of transportation connections

Passeig de Gràcia—Eixample, Block of Discord, transfer to the L2 (purple) line to Sagrada Família

Diagonal—Casa Milà

The L4 (yellow) line is also useful, with stops at Joanic (bus #116 to Park Güell), Jaume I (near Plaça de Sant Jaume and Picasso Museum), and Barceloneta (the harbor).

Practicalities

Barcelona's Public Transportation

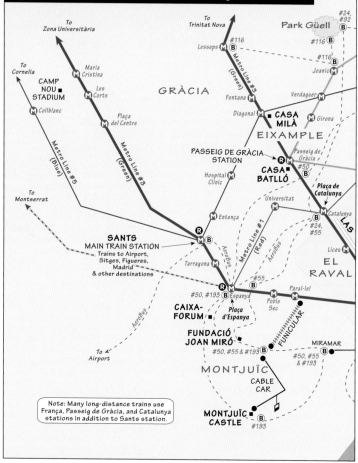

To Zona Universitària

To Trinitat Nova

Park Güell

#24, #92 B

Lesseps B #116

#116 B

Metro Line #3 (Green)

#116 B

Joanic M

To Cornella

CAMP NOU STADIUM

Maria Cristina M

Les Corts M

Collblanc M

GRÀCIA

Fontana M

Verdaguer B

Diagonal M CASA MILÀ

Girona M

EIXAMPLE

Plaça del Centre M

Metro Line #3 (Green)

PASSEIG DE GRÀCIA STATION

Passeig de Gràcia R M #50

Metro Line #5 (Blue)

CASA BATLLÓ

Plaça de Catalunya

To Montserrat

Hospital Clinic

Universitat M

Catalunya B

LAS

#24, #55

Entença M

SANTS MAIN TRAIN STATION
Trains to Airport, Sitges, Figueres, Madrid & other destinations

R M B

Metro Line #1 (Red)

AeroBús

Liceu B

EL RAVAL

Tarragona M

AeroBús

#55 B

CAIXA-FORUM ■

R #50, #193 B Espanya

Plaça d'Espanya

Poble Sec M

Paral·lel M

AeroBús

To Airport

FUNDACIÓ JOAN MIRÓ ■

#50, #55 & #193 B

FUNICULAR

MIRAMAR B

#50, #55 & #193 B

MONTJUÏC

CABLE CAR

MONTJUÏC CASTLE B

#193

Note: Many long-distance trains use França, Passeig de Gràcia, and Catalunya stations in addition to Sants station.

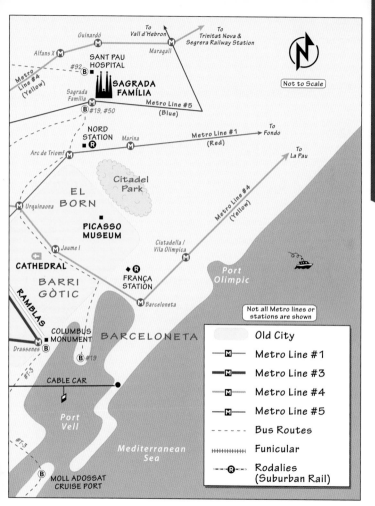

By Taxi

Barcelona is one of Europe's best taxi towns. Taxis are plentiful, the rates are clearly posted in every cab, and prices are reasonable. Flag down any cab with its green rooftop light on. By day (7:00-21:00) they charge *Tarif 2* (€1/kilometer plus €2.50 drop charge). You'll pay more after hours *(Tarif 1)*, for luggage, and surcharges to/from the train station or airport. A typical ride from Sants station to the Ramblas costs about €10.

By Bus

Given the excellent Metro service, it's unlikely you'll spend much time on local buses (also €2, covered by T10 Card, insert ticket in machine behind driver). However, buses can be handy for visiting Park Güell, Montjuïc, and the beach. More useful are the **hop-on hop-off tour buses** (✪ see page 184).

By Bike

Barcelona's traffic is probably too stressful to use a bike for most point-to-point travel. But joy-riding is wonderful in the Eixample, in Citadel Park, and along the Barceloneta beach. If you want to try biking but are intimidated by the traffic, consider taking a bike tour (described later, under "Activities").

Several places rent bikes for around €5 per hour (cheaper for longer rentals, may require a deposit). In the Old City, there's the helpful Un Cotxe Menys, near the Church of Santa Maria del Mar at Carrer de l'Esparteria 3 (tel. 932-682-105, www.bicicletabarcelona.com). Barcelona Rent-A-Bike is three blocks downhill from Plaça de Catalunya at Carrer dels Tallers 45 (tel. 933-171-970). On the Barceloneta beach, there's Biciclot, at Passeig Maritime 33 (tel. 932-219-778). In Citadel Park there are several rental places. Elsewhere, you'll see racks of government-subsidized "Bicing" borrow-a-bikes—but these are only for locals, not tourists.

COMMUNICATING

Telephones

Making Calls: To call Spain from the US or Canada: Dial 011-34 and then the local number (011 is our international access code; 34 is Spain's country code).

To call Spain from a European country: Dial 00-34 followed by the local number (00 is Europe's international access code).

To call within Spain, just dial the local number (Spain does not use area codes). If you're using your US mobile phone in Spain, you may need to call as if from the US—try it both ways.

To call from Spain to another country: Dial 00, the country code (for example, 1 for the US or Canada), the area code, and number. If you're calling European countries whose phone numbers begin with 0, you'll usually have to omit that 0 when you dial.

Phoning Inexpensively: Since coin-op pay phones are virtually obsolete, you'll need a phone card. The best option is a €5 international phone card (*tarjeta telefónica con código*), which works with a scratch-to-reveal PIN code. This gives you pennies-per-minute rates on international calls, decent rates for calls within Italy, and can even be used from your hotel phone. Buy them at newsstands and hole-in-the-wall shops catering to immigrants. Calling from your hotel room can be a rip-off for long-distance calls unless you use an international phone card.

Mobile Phones: A mobile phone—whether your own from home if it'll work in Spain, or a European one you buy when you arrive—is handy but can be pricey. You'll find mobile-phone stores selling cheap models with prepaid minutes and SIM cards at the airport, train station, and throughout Barcelona.

If traveling with a smartphone, switch off data-roaming until you have free Wi-Fi. Make phone calls for free or cheaply using Skype, Google Talk, or FaceTime.

For more on the fast-changing world of telephones, talk to your service provider or see www.ricksteves.com/phoning.

Internet Access

Almost all hotels offer some form of Internet access—either a computer in the lobby or Wi-Fi. Most provide these services for free for a small fee. Otherwise, have your hotelier direct you to an Internet café. Navega Web

Practicalities

Useful Phone Numbers

Police: Tel. 091 or 092
Ambulance or any Emergency: Tel. 112
Directory Assistance: Tel. 11811 (€0.40/min) or 11818 (€0.55/call from private numbers, free from phone booths)
US Consulate: Tel. 932-802-227, after-hours emergency tel. 915-872-200, Passeig Reina Elisenda 23, http://barcelona.usconsulate.gov
Canadian Consulate: Tel. 932-703-614, after-hours emergency tel. in Ottawa—call collect 613-996-8885, Plaça de Catalunya 9, www.spain .gc.ca

(€2/hour) has hundreds of terminals (daily 10:00-23:00, across from La Boqueria Market at Ramblas 88-94, tel. 933-179-193). Note that many Catalunyan businesses now use the web address ".cat" rather than ".com" or ".es".

SIGHTSEEING TIPS

Make reservations to avoid lines. Avoid entrance lines of an hour or more at a few key sights by reserving online or by telephone. This is smart for the Picasso Museum (✪ get the details on page 64), Sagrada Família (✪ see page 94), Casa Batlló (✪ see page 120), and Casa Milà (✪ see page 121). Another line-skipping option is the...

Articket BCN Sightseeing Pass: For €30, you get admission to seven art museums, skipping the ticket-buying lines. It includes the recommended Picasso Museum, Casa Milà, Catalan Art Museum, and Fundació Joan Miró. If you visit even three museums, it's worth it. The pass is sold at participating museums and some TIs. For more info, see www.articket bcn.org.

On the other hand, I'd skip the Barcelona Card, which covers public transportation and a few minor sights.

Hours: Since opening hours can change year-to-year, it's always wise to get the most up-to-date at the TI or www.barcelonaturisme.com.

Be aware that many top sights are closed on Monday—making them especially crowded on Tuesday and Sunday.

Typical Rules: Some sights have metal detectors or conduct bag searches that will slow your entry. Some don't allow large bags and may not allow you to bring liquids (water bottles) in. Photos and videos are normally allowed, but flashes or tripods usually are not.

Discounts: Many sights offer discounts for youths (up to age 18), students (with proper identification cards, www.isic.org), families, seniors (loosely defined as retirees or those willing to call themselves seniors), and groups of 10 or more. Always ask. Some discounts are only for EU citizens.

Pace Yourself: Schedule cool breaks into your sightseeing where you can sit and refresh with a drink or snack.

THEFT AND EMERGENCIES

While violent crime is rare, thieves (mainly pickpockets) thrive in crowds. Be alert to the possibility of theft, especially when you're absorbed in the wonder and newness of Barcelona. You're more likely to be pickpocketed in Barcelona—especially along the Ramblas—than just about anywhere else in Europe. Thieves zipping by on motorbikes grab handbags from pedestrians. Leave valuables in your hotel and wear a money belt.

Here are some common scams: "police officers" looking for counterfeit bills; a too-friendly local who engages you in conversation while he picks your pocket; thieves posing as lost tourists who ask for your help; street gamblers playing the pea-and-carrot game (a variation on the shell game); and groups of women aggressively "selling carnations," while actually rifling your pocket. If you encounter any commotion or distraction on the Ramblas, put your hands in your pockets before someone else does.

Some neighborhoods feel seedy and can be unsafe after dark. I'd avoid the lower part of the Barri Gòtic southeast of Plaça Reial (though the strip near the Carrer de la Mercè tapas bars is better). Don't venture too deep into the Raval (just west of the Ramblas)—one block can separate a comfy tourist zone from the junkies and prostitutes.

Emergency Help: Dial 091 or 092 for police help or 112 for any emergency (medical or otherwise).

Lost or Stolen Items: To replace a passport, contact an embassy or consulate (for contact info, ✪ see page 178). File a police report without delay; it's required to submit an insurance claim for lost or stolen railpasses or travel gear, and can help with replacing your passport or credit and debit cards. For more information, see www.ricksteves.com/help.

Medical Help: If you get sick, do as the Spanish do and go to a pharmacist for advice. There's a 24-hour pharmacy across from La Boqueria Market at Ramblas #98, and another near Casa Milà. Or ask at your hotel for help finding medical services.

ACTIVITIES

Shopping

Whatever your taste or budget, Barcelona is a good shopping city. The streets of the Barri Gòtic and El Born are bursting with characteristic hole-in-the-wall shops, while the Eixample is the upscale "uptown" shopping district. Near Plaça de Catalunya, Avinguda Portal de l'Angel has a staggering array of department and chain stores.

Souvenir Items: In this artistic city, consider picking up Picasso prints, Dalí posters, Miró mouse pads, and books about Gaudí. Museum gift shops (Picasso Museum and Casa Milà) are a bonanza for art lovers. Home-decor shops have Euro-style housewares unavailable back home and Modernista-flavored glassware. Decorative tile and pottery (popularized by Modernist architects) and Modernista jewelry are easy to pack. Foodies might bring back olive oil, wine, spices (such as saffron or sea salts), cheese, or the local nougat treat, torró. (See below for US customs rules on foods.) An *espadenya*—or *espadrille* in Spanish—is the trendy canvas-and-rope shoe that originated as humble Catalan peasant footwear. For a souvenir of Catalan culture, consider a Catalan flag, a dragon of St. Jordi, or a jersey or scarf from the wildly popular Barça soccer team.

Sizes: European clothing sizes are different from the US. For example, a woman's size 10 dress (US) is a European size 40, and a size 8 shoe (US) is a European size 38-39.

Getting a VAT Refund: If you spend more than €90 on goods at a single store, you may be eligible to get a refund of the 21 percent Value-Added Tax (VAT). You'll need to ask the merchant to fill out the necessary refund document, then process your refund through a service such as Global Blue or Premier Tax Free, with offices at major airports. For more details, see www.ricksteves.com/vat.

Customs for American Shoppers: You are allowed to take home $800 worth of items per person duty-free, once every 30 days. You can also bring in duty-free a liter of alcohol. As for food, you can take home many processed and packaged foods (e.g., vacuum-packed cheeses, chocolate, mustard) but no fresh produce or meats. Any liquid-containing foods must be packed (carefully) in checked luggage. To check customs rules and duty rates, visit www.cbp.gov.

Shopping Neighborhoods

Barri Gòtic: Stroll from the cathedral to the Ramblas, through interesting streets lined with little local shops. Avoid the midafternoon siesta and Sundays, when many shops are closed.

Face the cathedral, turn 90 degrees right, and exit Plaça Nova (just to the left of the Bilbao Berria restaurant) on the tight lane called Carrer de la Palla. This street has a half-dozen antique shops crammed with moth-balled treasures. Mixed in are a few art galleries, offbeat shops, and a motorcycle museum. When you reach the fork in the road (where the inviting Caelum café is), take the right fork. You'll pass by Oro Líquido ("Liquid Gold"), selling high-quality olive oils.

You'll soon reach the Church of Santa Maria del Pi ringed by a charming, café-lined square. Skirt around the right side of the church to find Josep Roca, a genteel gentleman's shop, and Vaho selling recycled "trashion bags."

From the Josep Roca shop, head up narrow Carrer Petritxol ("peht-ree-CHUHL"). It's a fun combination of art galleries, fancy jewelry shops, and simple local places for hot chocolate and churros (check out Granja La Pallaresa, just after #11).

You'll dead-end onto Carrer de la Portaferrissa, with its international teen clothing stores. From here, you can turn left to reach the Ramblas, or turn right to return to the cathedral.

Eixample: This ritzy "uptown" district is home to some of the city's top-end shops. From Plaça de Catalunya, head north up Passeig de Gràcia. You'll pass by lower-end international stores (like Zara) at the lower end of the street, to top-end brands at the top (Gucci, Luis Vuitton, Escada, Chanel). Near Casa Milà, check out Vinçon (Passeig de Gràcia 96, www.vincon.com), a sprawling Euro-housewares store that feels like a trendy Spanish Ikea. Detour one block west to Rambla de Catalunya, with more local (but still expensive) options.

El Born: For a nice route through this boutique-speckled neighborhood, ✪ see the El Born Walk (page 115).

Placa de Catalunya and Avinguda Portal de l'Angel: Barcelona natives do most of their shopping at big department stores. Get a sense of contemporary Spanish fashion by strolling down the street that runs south from Placa de Catalunya. El Corte Inglés is the Spanish answer to one-stop shopping—everything from clothes to furniture to electronics, bonsai trees, a travel agency, groceries, and haircuts. The Spanish chain Zara and Barcelona-based Mango focus on clothes. Women's Secret is the Spanish answer to Victoria's Secret, Pull and Bear is the Spanish Gap, and Kemper does shoes. Also along the street are numerous international chains, from the teen-oriented French chain Pimkie to Italy's Intimissimi, to conglomerates like H&M, Esprit, and Benetton.

Nightlife

For their evening entertainment, Barcelonans stroll the streets, greeting neighbors, popping into a bar for drinks and tapas, nursing a cocktail on a floodlit square, or enjoying a late meal. Dinnertime is around 22:00, and even families with children can be out well after midnight. The liveliest neighborhoods are the funky El Born, the ritzy Eixample, the touristy Barri Gòtic, and the always-crowded Ramblas.

In addition, Barcelona always has a vast array of cultural events. Pick up the TI's free monthly English-language magazine, *In BCN Culture & Leisure*. Another good source of information is the Palau de la Virreina ticket office (Ramblas 99, tel. 933-161-000). Or check www.barcelona cultura.bcn.cat or www.barcelonaplanning.com.

You can buy tickets directly from the venue, from box offices at El Corte Inglés or the FNAC store (both on Plaça de Catalunya), from Palau de Verreina, or at www.ticketmaster.es or www.telentrada.com.

Live Music: The Palace of Catalan Music (Palau de la Música Catalana), with one of the finest Modernista interiors in town (✪ see listing on page 114), offers everything from symphonic to Catalan folk songs to chamber music to flamenco (€22-49 tickets, Carrer Palau de la Música 4-6, Metro: Urquinaona, tel. 902-442-882, www.palaumusica.cat).

The Liceu Opera House (Gran Teatre del Liceu), right in the heart of the Ramblas, is a sumptuous venue for opera, dance, and concerts (tickets from €10, La Rambla 51-59, box office just around the corner at Carrer Sant Pau 1, Metro: Liceu, tel. 934-859-913, www.liceubarcelona.cat).

Other classy venues occasionally hosting concerts are Casa Milà (www.lapedrera.com), Fundació Joan Miró (www.fundaciomiro-bcn .org), and CaixaForum (http://obrasocial.lacaixa.es—choose "CaixaForum Barcelona").

"Masters of Guitar" concerts are offered nearly nightly at 21:00 in the Barri Gòtic's Church of Santa Maria del Pi (€21 at the door, Plaça del Pi 7, tel. 647-514-513, www.maestrosdelaguitarra.com).

Though flamenco music is not typical of Barcelona (it's from Andalucía), you'll find entertaining concerts nightly at Tarantos, on Plaça Reial (at #17, tel. 933-191-789, www.masimas.com/en/tarantos, or just drop by for tickets).

Casa Milà hosts the "Summer Nights at La Pedrera" concerts (mostly jazz) on its fanciful floodlit rooftop, weekends from June to September (book ahead at tel. 902-101-212 or www.lapedrera.com).

Hotel Casa Fuster, a Modernista landmark, has jazz every Thursday at 21:00 (€15 "membership" required, reservations recommended, north of Avinguda Diagonal at Passeig de Gràcia 132, tel. 932-553-006, cafevienesjazzclub.blogspot.com).

Jamboree, right on Plaça Reial, has jazz nightly at 20:00 and 22:00 in its cellar (€5-10 in advance or at the door, Plaça Reial 17, tel. 933-191-789, www.masimas.com/en/jamboree).

Evening Sightseeing: For a list of sights open in the evening (19:30 or later), ✪ see page 11. The hop-on, hop-off Tourist Bus runs until 20:00 daily in summer. The illuminated Magic Fountains on Montjuïc also make a good finale for your day.

After-Hours Neighborhoods

Join bar-hopping Barcelonans for tapas, drinks, and dancing into the wee hours. The weekend ritual (Thu-Sat) might go something like this: evening tapas; dinner at 22:00; a music club for cocktails and DJ music from mid-night; then, at about 2:00 or 3:00 in the morning, hit the discos until the sun comes up. The following neighborhoods party late, but they're also lively for tapas and drinks in the early evening.

El Born: Passeig del Born, a broad parklike strip stretching from the Church of Santa Maria del Mar, is lined with inviting bars and nightspots. Wander the side streets for more options. Miramelindo is a local favorite for mojitos (Passeig del Born 15). La Vinya del Senyor is mellower, for tapas and wine on the square in front of Santa Maria del Mar.

Practicalities

Plaça Reial (in the Barri Gòtic): A block off the Ramblas, this palm-tree-graced square bustles with trendy eateries charging inflated prices for pleasant outdoor tables—perfect for nursing a drink (try the Ocaña Bar at #13). Or buy a €1 beer from a convenience store and lean against a palm tree. Plaça Reial is also home to the Tarantos flamenco bar and Jamboree jazz club (both described earlier), plus the hip Sidecar Factory Club (at #7, often live music, www.sidecarfactoryclub.com) and the hidden, mellow, pipe-happy Barcelona Pipa Club (at #3—find and ring the doorbell to get inside, this member's club opens to the public around 22:00, www.bpipa club.com).

Carrer de la Mercè: This Barri Gòtic street near the harbor is lined with salty local tapas bars, with a few trendy ones mixed in (✪ see page 156).

The Eixample: Barcelona's upscale uptown is better for classy tapas in the evening than for after-midnight partying. For cocktail bars with breezy outdoor seating, try the parklike Rambla de Catalunya. A couple of blocks over, Carrer d'Enric Granados and Carrer d'Aribau draw the gay community.

Barceloneta: The broad beach is dotted with *chiringuitos*—shacks selling drinks and snacks, creating a fun, lively scene on a balmy summer evening. At the north end of the beach (in the former Olympic Village) are a number of trendy, exclusive, and expensive discos, including Opium Mar (www.opiummar.com). These places get going extremely late, and you must be "somebody" (or look good) to get in. I couldn't find a single place willing to check my rucksack.

Tours

Hop-on Hop-off Bus Tours: Double-decker buses give tourists a drive-by look at major landmarks while listening to recorded descriptions. In Barcelona, I use these not merely as an overview of the city, but also as handy transportation to out-of-the-way sights.

Tourist Bus (Bus Turístic) offers two main routes, centered on their hub on Plaça de Catalunya. The two-hour blue route (departing from near El Corte Inglés) covers north Barcelona (most Gaudí sights). The two-hour red route (from the west side of the Plaça) covers south Barcelona (Barri Gòtic and Montjuïc). One-day (€24) and two-day (€31) tickets also come with 10-20 percent discounts on major sights and walking tours. Buy tickets on the bus or at the TI. Tourist Bus operates daily 9:00-20:00 in summer, 9:00-19:00 in winter, www.barcelonabusturistic.cat).

A different company, Barcelona City Tour, offers a nearly identical service (www.barcelonacitytour.cat).

Walking Tours: Several companies take groups of 10-30 people on two-hour guided walks in English, giving a once-over of Barcelona's history, culture, and sights for around €15-20. You just show up at the meeting point and pay your fee (though reserving ahead is always smart). The TI at Plaça de Sant Jaume offers great guided walks through the Barri Gòtic (daily at 9:30, reserve a day ahead in summer, tel. 932-853-832, www .barcelonaturisme.cat). The TI at Plaça de Catalunya offers a number of theme walks: Picasso, gourmet walks, Modernisme, and more.

Some companies offer "free" walks that rely on—and expect—a tip at the end. For these, I tip €5 minimum, and up to €15 for excellence. Try Runner Bean Tours (mobile 636-108-776, www.runnerbeantours.com) or Discover Walks (tel. 931-816-810, www.discoverwalks.com).

For around €200, you can hire your own private guide for a few hours. Try the Barcelona Guide Bureau (tel. 932-682-422, www.bgb.es) or José Soler (mobile 615-059-326, www.pepitotours.com).

Guided Bus Tours: Several companies offer bus tours of Barcelona with an English-speaking guide for around €50. These can be handy for reaching outlying sights (such Sagrada Família or Park Güell) or day-trip destinations (Montserrat or Figueres). Try the Barcelona Guide Bureau (tel. 933-152-261, www.barcelonaguidebureau.com) or Catalunya Tourist Bus (tel. 932-853-832, www.catalunyabusturistic.com).

Bike Tours: A fun way to see the city is with a group of other cyclists on rental bikes (around €20-25). Near Plaça Sant Jaume, try Un Cotxe Menys ("One Car Less," tel. 932-682-105, www.bicicletabarcelona.com). At Plaça de Catalunya, try Barcelona CicloTour (tel. 933-171-970, www .barcelonaciclotour.com).

RESOURCES FROM RICK STEVES

This Pocket guide is one of more than 30 titles in my series of guidebooks on European travel. I also produce a public television series, *Rick Steves' Europe,* and a public radio show, *Travel with Rick Steves.*

My website, www.ricksteves.com, offers a wealth of free travel resources, including my Rick Steves Audio Europe app (featuring audio tours of Europe's greatest sights, museums and neighborhoods), a Travelers Helpline forum, guidebook updates, and my travel blog—plus my travel gear store and information on rail passes and our tours of Europe.

How was your trip? If you'd like to share your tips, concerns, and discoveries after using this book, please fill out the survey at www.rick steves.com/feedback. It helps us and fellow travelers.

Spanish Survival Phrases

In the phonetics, the italicized *h* sounds like the gutteral **j** in Baja California.

English	Spanish	Phonetics
Good day.	Buenos días.	**bway**-nohs dee-ahs
Do you speak English?	¿Habla Usted inglés?	**ah**-blah oo-**stehd** een-**glays**
Yes. / No.	Sí. / No.	see / noh
I (don't) understand.	(No) comprendo.	(noh) kohm-**prehn**-doh
Please.	Por favor.	por fah-**bor**
Thank you.	Gracias.	**grah**-thee-ahs
I'm sorry.	Lo siento.	loh see-**ehn**-toh
Excuse me.	Perdóneme.	pehr-**doh**-nay-may
(No) problem.	(No) problema.	(noh) proh-**blay**-mah
Good.	Bueno.	**bway**-noh
Goodbye.	Adiós.	ah-dee-**ohs**
one / two	uno / dos	**oo**-noh / dohs
three / four	tres / cuatro	trays / **kwah**-troh
five / six	cinco / seis	**theen**-koh / says
seven / eight	siete / ocho	see-**eh**-tay / **oh**-choh
nine / ten	nueve / diez	**nway**-bay / dee-**ayth**
How much is it?	¿Cuánto cuesta?	**kwahn**-toh **kway**-stah
Write it?	¿Me lo escribe?	may loh ay-**skree**-bay
Is it free?	¿Es gratis?	ays **grah**-tees
Is it included?	¿Está incluido?	ay-**stah** een-kloo-**ee**-doh
Where can I buy / find...?	¿Dónde puedo comprar / encontrar...?	**dohn**-day **pway**-doh kohm-**prar** / ayn-kohn-**trar**
I'd like / We'd like...	Quiero / Queremos...	kee-**ehr**-oh / kehr-**ay**-mohs
...a room.	...una habitación.	**oo**-nah ah-bee-tah-thee-**ohn**
...a ticket to ___.	...un billete para ___.	oon bee-**yeh**-tay **pah**-rah ___
Where is...?	¿Dónde está...?	**dohn**-day ay-**stah**
...the train station	...la estación de trenes	lah ay-stah-thee-**ohn** day **tray**-nays
...the tourist information office	...la oficina de turismo	lah oh-fee-**thee**-nah day too-**rees**-moh
Where are the toilets?	¿Dónde están los servicios?	**dohn**-day ay-**stahn** lohs sehr-**bee**-thee-ohs
men	hombres, caballeros	**ohm**-brays, kah-bah-**yay**-rohs
women	mujeres, damas	moo-*heh*-rays, **dah**-mahs
left / right	izquierda / derecha	eeth-kee-**ehr**-dah / day-**ray**-chah
straight	derecho	day-**ray**-choh
When do you open / close?	¿A qué hora abren / cierran?	ah kay **oh**-rah **ah**-brehn / thee-**ay**-rahn
At what time?	¿A qué hora?	ah kay **oh**-rah
Just a moment.	Un momento.	oon moh-**mehn**-toh
now / soon / later	ahora / pronto / más tarde	ah-**oh**-rah / **prohn**-toh / mahs **tar**-day
today / tomorrow	hoy / mañana	oy / mahn-**yah**-nah

In a Spanish Restaurant

English	Spanish	Pronunciation
I'd like / We'd like...	Quiero / Queremos...	kee-**ehr**-oh / kehr-**ay**-mohs
...to reserve...	...reservar...	ray-sehr-**bar**
...a table for	...una mesa para	oo-nah **may**-sah **pah**-rah
one / two.	uno / dos.	**oo**-noh / dohs
Is this table free?	¿Está esta mesa libre?	ay-**stah** ay-stah **may**-sah lee-**bray**
The menu (in English),please.	La carta (en inglés), por favor.	lah **kar**-tah (ayn een-**glays**) por fah-**bor**
service (not) included	servicio (no) incluido	sehr-**bee**-thee-oh (noh) een-kloo-**ee**-doh
to go	para llevar	**pah**-rah yay-**bar**
with / without	con / sin	kohn / seen
and / or	y / o	ee / oh
fixed-price meal (of the day)	menú (del día)	may-**noo** (dayl **dee**-ah)
specialty of the house	especialidad de la casa	ay-spay-thee-ah-lee-**dahd** day lah **kah**-sah
combination plate	plato combinado	**plah**-toh kohm-bee-**nah**-doh
appetizers	tapas	**tah**-pahs
bread	pan	pahn
cheese	queso	**kay**-soh
sandwich	bocadillo	boh-kah-**dee**-yoh
soup	sopa	**soh**-pah
salad	ensalada	ayn-sah-**lah**-dah
meat	carne	**kar**-nay
poultry	aves	**ah**-bays
fish	pescado	pay-**skah**-doh
seafood	marisco	mah-**ree**-skoh
dessert	postres	**poh**-strays
tap water	agua del grifo	**ah**-gwah dayl **gree**-foh
mineral water	agua mineral	**ah**-gwah mee-nay-**rahl**
milk	leche	**lay**-chay
(orange) juice	zumo (de naranja)	**thoo**-moh (day nah-**rahn**-hah)
coffee / tea	café / té	kah-**feh** / tay
wine	vino	**bee**-noh
red / white	tinto / blanco	**teen**-toh / **blahn**-koh
glass / bottle	vaso / botella	**bah**-soh / boh-**tay**-yah
beer	cerveza	thehr-**bay**-thah
Cheers!	¡Salud!	sah-**lood**
More. / Another.	Más. / Otro.	mahs / **oh**-troh
The same.	El mismo.	ehl **mees**-moh
The bill, please.	La cuenta, por favor.	lah **kwayn**-tah por fah-**bor**
tip	propina	proh-**pee**-nah
Delicious!	¡Delicioso!	day-lee-thee-**oh**-soh

For many more phrases, check out *Rick Steves' Spanish Phrase Book*.

Catalan Survival Phrases

English	Catalan	Pronunciation
Hello.	Hola.	**oh**-lah
Do you speak English?	Parla anglès?	**par**-lah ahn-**glays**
Yes. / No.	Sí. / No.	see / noh
I (don't) understand.	(No) entenc.	(noh) ahn-**tehnk**
Please.	Si us plau.	see oos plow
Thank you (very much).	(Moltes) Gràcies.	(**mohl**-tahs) **grah**-see-ahs
I'm sorry.	Ho sento.	oo **sehn**-too
Excuse me.	Perdó.	pahr-**doh**
(No) problem.	(Cap) problema.	(kahp) pruh-**bleh**-mah
Good.	Bé.	bay
Goodbye.	Adéu.	ah-**day**-oo
one / two	un / dos	oon / dohs
three / four	tres / quatre	trehs / **kwah**-trah
five / six	cinc / sis	seenk / sees
seven / eight	set / vuit	seht / **voo**-eet
nine / ten	nou / deu	**noh**-oo / **deh**-oo
How much?	Quant és?	kwahn ehs
Write it?	M'ho escriu?	moh ah-**skree**-oo
Is it free?	És gratis?	ehs **grah**-tees
Is it included?	Està inclós?	ah-**stah** ihn-**klohs**
Where can I find / buy...?	On puc trobar / comprar...?	ohn pook troo-**bah** / koom-**prah**
I'd like...	Voldria...	vool-**dree**-ah
We'd like...	Voldríem...	vool-**dree**-ahm
...a room.	...una habitació	oo-nah ah-bee-tah-see-**oh**
...a ticket to ___.	...una entrada per ___.	oo-nah ahn-**trah**-dah pahr ___
Where is...?	On està...?	ohn ah-**stah**
...the train station	...l'estació del tren	lah-stah-see-**oh** dahl trehn
...the tourist information office	...l'oficina de turisme	loo-fee-**see**-nah dah too-**reez**-mah
...the toilet	...els serveis	ahls sahr-**vays**
men / women	homes / dones	**oh**-mahs / **doh**-nahs
left / right	esquerre / dreta	ahs-**keh**-reh / **dreh**-tah
straight	dret	dreht
At what time...?	A quina hora...?	ah **kee**-nah oh-rah
...does this open / close	...obre / tanca	**oh**-brah / **tahn**-kah
Just a moment.	Un moment.	oon moo-**mehn**
now / soon / later	ara / aviat / més tard	**ah**-rah / ah-vee-**aht** / mehs tahrd
today / tomorrow	avui / demà	ah-**vwee** / dah-**mah**
Long live Catalunya!	¡Visca Catalunya!	**vee**-skah kah-tah-**loon**-yah

In the Catalan Restaurant

I'd like to reserve...	**Voldria reservar...**	vool-**dree**-ah rah-sahr-**vah**
We'd like to reserve...	**Voldríem reservar...**	vool-**dree**-ahm rah-sahr-**vah**
...a table for one / two	**...una taula per una / dues**	oo-nah **tow**-lah pahr oo-nah / doo-**ehs**
Is this table free?	**Està lliure aquesta taula?**	ah-**stah** yoo-rah ah-**kwehs**-tah **tow**-lah
The menu (in English), please.	**La carta (en anglès), si us plau.**	lah **kar**-tah (ahn ahn-**glays**) see oos plow
service (not) included	**servei (no) inclós**	sahr-**vay**ee (noh) ihn-**klohs**
to go	**per emportar**	pahr ahm-por-**tah**
with / without	**amb / sense**	ahm / **sehn**-sah
and / or	**i / o**	ee / oh
tapas (small plates)	**tapes**	**tah**-pahs
fixed-price meal (of the day)	**menú (del dia)**	mah-**noo** (dahl **dee**-ah)
daily special	**plat del dia**	plaht dahl **dee**-ah
specialty of the house	**especialitat de la casa**	ah-spah-see-ah-lee-**taht** dah lah **kah**-zah
combination plate	**plat combinat**	plaht koom-bee-**naht**
appetizers	**entrants**	ahn-**trahns**
bread	**pà**	pah
cheese	**formatge**	foor-**mah**-jah
sandwich	**entrepà**	ahn-trah-**pah**
soup	**sopa**	**soh**-pah
salad	**amanida**	ah-mah-**nee**-dah
meat	**carn**	karn
poultry	**aviram**	ah-vee-**rahm**
fish	**peix**	paysh
seafood	**marisc**	mah-**reesk**
dessert	**postres**	**poh**-strahs
(tap) water	**aigua (de l'aixeta)**	**eye**-wah (dah lah-**shay**-tah)
mineral water	**aigua mineral**	**eye**-wah mee-nah-**rahl**
milk	**llet**	yeht
(orange) juice	**suc (de taronja)**	sook (dah tah-**rohn**-zhah)
coffee / tea	**cafè / te**	kah-**feh** / teh
wine	**vi**	vee
red / white	**negre / blanc**	**neh**-grah / blahnk
sweet / dry / semi-dry	**dolç / sec / semi-sec**	dohls / sehk / **seh**-mee sehk
glass / bottle	**copa / ampolla**	**koh**-pah / ahm-**poy**-yah
beer	**cervesa**	sahr-**veh**-zah
Cheers!	**Salut!**	sah-**looy**
More. / Another.	**Més. / Un altre.**	mehs / oon **ahl**-trah
The same.	**El mateix.**	ahl mah-**taysh**
the bill	**el compte**	ahl **kohmp**-tah
tip	**propina**	proo-**pee**-nah
Delicious!	**Boníssim!**	boo-**nee**-seem

Practicalities

INDEX

Index

Index

Audio Europe

Rick's Free Travel App

Get your FREE **Rick Steves Audio Europe**™ app to enjoy...

- Dozens of self-guided tours of Europe's top museums, sights and historic walks
- Hundreds of tracks filled with cultural insights and sightseeing tips from Rick's radio interviews
- All organized into handy geographic playlists
- For iPhone, iPad, iPod Touch, Android

With Rick whispering in your ear, Europe gets even better.

Find out more at ricksteves.com

Start your trip at

Free information and great gear to

▸ Plan Your Trip

Browse thousands of articles and a wealth of money-saving tips for planning your dream trip. You'll find up-to-date information on Europe's best destinations, packing smart, getting around, finding rooms, staying healthy, avoiding scams and more.

▸ Eurail Passes

Find out, step-by-step, if a railpass makes sense for your trip—and how to avoid buying more than you need. Get a bunch of free extras!

▸ Graffiti Wall & Travelers Helpline

Learn, ask, share—our online community of savvy travelers is a great resource for first-time travelers to Europe, as well as seasoned pros.

Rick Steves' Europe Through the Back Door, Inc.

Rick Steves® www.ricksteves.com

EUROPE GUIDES

Best of Europe
Eastern Europe
Europe Through the Back Door
Mediterranean Cruise Ports

COUNTRY GUIDES

Croatia & Slovenia
England
France
Germany
Great Britain
Ireland
Italy
Portugal
Scandinavia
Spain
Switzerland

CITY & REGIONAL GUIDES

Amsterdam, Bruges & Brussels
Barcelona
Budapest
Florence & Tuscany
Greece: Athens & the Peloponnese
Istanbul
London
Paris
Prague & the Czech Republic
Provence & the French Riviera
Rome
Venice
Vienna, Salzburg & Tirol

SNAPSHOT GUIDES

Berlin
Bruges & Brussels
Copenhagen & the Best of Denmark
Dublin
Dubrovnik
Hill Towns of Central Italy
Italy's Cinque Terre
Krakow, Warsaw & Gdansk
Lisbon
Madrid & Toledo
Munich, Bavaria & Salzburg
Naples & the Amalfi Coast
Northern Ireland
Norway
Scotland
Sevilla, Granada & Southern Spain
Stockholm

POCKET GUIDES

Athens
Barcelona
Florence
London
Paris
Rome
Venice

TRAVEL CULTURE

Europe 101
European Christmas
Postcards from Europe
Travel as a Political Act

NOW AVAILABLE:
eBOOKS, DVD & BLU-RAY

eBOOKS

Nearly all Rick Steves guides are available as eBooks. Check with your favorite bookseller.

RICK STEVES' EUROPE DVDS

10 New Shows 2011–2012
Austria & the Alps
Eastern Europe
England & Wales
European Christmas
European Travel Skills & Specials
France
Germany, BeNeLux & More
Greece & Turkey
Iran
Ireland & Scotland
Italy's Cities
Italy's Countryside
Scandinavia
Spain
Travel Extras

BLU-RAY

Celtic Charms
Eastern Europe Favorites
European Christmas
Italy Through the Back Door
Mediterranean Mosaic
Surprising Cities of Europe

PHRASE BOOKS & DICTIONARIES

French
French, Italian & German
German
Italian
Portuguese
Spanish

JOURNALS

Rick Steves' Pocket Travel Journal
Rick Steves' Travel Journal

PLANNING MAPS

Britain, Ireland & London
Europe
France & Paris
Germany, Austria & Switzerland
Ireland
Italy
Spain & Portugal

Rick Steves guidebooks are published by Avalon Travel, a member of the Perseus Books Group.
Rick Steves books and DVDs are available at bookstores and through online booksellers.

PHOTO CREDITS

Eixample Walk

© Cameron Hewitt, Suzanne Kotz, Robyn Stencil; additional images from Wikimedia Commons

Sagrada Família Tour

© Cameron Hewitt, Rick Steves

Sights

© Cameron Hewitt, Rick Steves, Robyn Stencil; additional images from Wikimedia Commons

Sleeping

© Robyn Stencil, Dominic Bonuccelli

Eating

© Suzanne Kotz, Rick Steves

Practicalities

© Cameron Hewitt, Rick Steves

Avalon Travel
a member of the Perseus Books Group
1700 Fourth Street
Berkeley, CA 94710, USA

Printed in China by RR Donnelley
First printing June 2013

ISBN 978-1-61238-553-2
ISSN 2326-1994

For the latest on Rick's lectures, books, tours, public-radio show, and public-television
series, contact Europe Through the Back Door, Box 2009, Edmonds, WA 98020, tel.
425/771-8303, fax 425/771-0833, www.ricksteves.com, rick@ricksteves.com.

Europe Through the Back Door
Managing Editor: Risa Laib
Editors: Jennifer Madison Davis, Glenn Eriksen, Tom Griffin, Cameron Hewitt,
    Suzanne Kotz, Cathy Lu, Gretchen Strauch
Editorial Interns: Emily Dugdale, Jessica Shaw
Researcher: Cameron Hewitt
Graphic Content Director: Laura VanDeventer
Maps & Graphics: David C. Hoerlein, Twozdai Hulse, Lauren Mills

Avalon Travel
Senior Editor and Series Manager: Madhu Prasher
Editor: Jamie Andrade
Assistant Editor: Nikki Ioakimedes
Copy Editor: Denise Silva
Proofreader: Kelly Lydick
Indexer: Stephen Callahan
Production & Typesetting: McGuire Barber Design
Cover Design: Kimberly Glyder Design
Maps & Graphics: Kat Bennett, Mike Morgenfeld

ABOUT THE AUTHORS

Rick Steves
Rick writes a bestselling guidebook series; produces a public television series *(Rick Steves' Europe)*, public radio show *(Travel with Rick Steves)*, and an app and podcast *(Rick Steves Audio Europe)*; and organizes guided tours that take over 10,000 travelers to Europe annually. Rick's mission is to make European travel fun, affordable, and culturally enlightening for Americans.

Connect with Rick:

facebook.com/RickSteves twitter: @RickSteves

Gene Openshaw
Gene is a writer, composer, tour guide, and lecturer on art and history. Specializing in writing walking tours of Europe's cultural sights, Gene is the co-author of 10 Rick Steves' guidebooks and contributes to Rick's public television series. He lives near Seattle with his daughter and roots for the Mariners in good times and bad.

Cameron Hewitt
Cameron writes and edits guidebooks for Rick Steves, specializing in Eastern Europe. For this book, he gorged on Gaudí, bored into El Born, marveled at Miró, aced the Eixample, and sashayed the *sardana* in front of the cathedral. When he's not traveling, Cameron lives in Seattle with his wife Shawna.

FOLDOUT COLOR MAP

The foldout map on the opposite page includes:

• Maps of Barcelona on one side

• Maps of Barcelona and Spain on the other side